RETURN TO GLORY

THE STORY OF ALABAMA'S 2008 SEASON

KCI Sports Publishing
3340 Whiting Avenue, Suite 5
Stevens Point, WI 54481
Phone: 1-800-697-3756
Fax: 715-344-2668

HTTP://WWW.KCISPORTS.COM/ | PUBLISHER: PETER J. CLARK

ISBN: 978-0-9798729-3-8 (hard cover) ISBN: 978-0-9798729-4-5 (soft cover)
Printed in the United States

ACKNOWLEDGEMENTS

Design Editor: Janet Sudnik
Editorial Content Editor: Tommy Deas
Photo Editor: Robert Sutton

Content for this book was taken from coverage of the University of Alabama's 2008 football season in the pages of The Tuscaloosa News, with a few extra stories produced for this publication.

Game stories and features were written by Cecil Hurt, Tommy Deas and Chris Walsh, with editorial support from Aaron Suttles and Andrew Carroll.

Photos were taken by Robert Sutton, Dusty Compton, Dan Lopez, Michael E. Palmer and Jason Harless.

The Tuscaloosa News staff file photo

The Tuscaloosa News
315 28TH AVENUE | TUSCALOOSA, AL | 35401

FORWARD

There were expectations for the University of Alabama football team at the start of the 2008 season. There always are high hopes among Crimson Tide fans. But there also seemed to be a sense that, while big things were on the horizon, this wouldn't be the season in which the loftiest dreams would be realized.

Instead, Alabama arrived — or came within inches of arriving — ahead of schedule.

There were numerous reasons for that. The coaching of Nick Saban was a key ingredient. But, as most successful head coaches do, Saban deflected the acclaim to his players. In that area, the Crimson Tide drew upon its veteran players and its newcomers in equal measure.

On the offensive side of the ball, senior quarterback John Parker Wilson had the best year of his career. Running back Glen Coffee, a junior, burst into stardom. Tackle Andre Smith fulfilled all the expectations that have accompanied his career, winning the Outland Trophy as the nation's best interior lineman. Senior center Antoine Caldwell nearly matched that, earning All-America honors. Freshman Julio Jones proved to be the perfect addition for providing a big-play threat. On defense, newcomers Terrence Cody and Dont'a Hightower blended almost perfectly with veterans like Bobby Greenwood, Rolando McClain and Rashad Johnson.

The result was a perfect 12-0 run through the regular season and a strong run at Florida in the Southeastern Conference title game, a challenge that just fell short in the fourth quarter.

Ultimately, 2008 proved, in some ways, to be what was expected — a step toward the ultimate destination of championship status. But it was a much longer step in that direction than anyone originally expected.

CECIL HURT
Sports Editor
The Tuscaloosa News

RETURN TO GLORY | CONTENTS

Cover photo: *The Tuscaloosa News | Jason Harless*
Back cover photo: *The Tuscaloosa News | Michael E. Palmer*

PROLOGUE

This page: Fans and media cheer and crowd around to greet UA's then-new head football coach, Nick Saban, on Jan. 3, 2007.
The Tuscaloosa News | Michael E. Palmer

Nick Saban made it clear from the day he arrived that the Alabama Crimson Tide's return to football glory would not be an event as much as a process. The 27th head coach in Alabama's storied gridiron history arrived on Jan. 3, 2007, to a raucous greeting from overjoyed fans at Tuscaloosa's airport.

Saban came to Alabama with a national championship ring from his tenure as LSU's head coach and a reputation as one of the most able football minds in America. A few months later, more than 100,000 showed up at the A-Day spring football game, with thousands turned away after Bryant-Denny Stadium filled beyond its capacity.

The process, however, was not a smooth ride from the start. Saban's first season started well enough, with the Crimson Tide winning six of its first eight games and defeating rival Tennessee soundly, 41-17, but player suspensions for violation of team rules and off-the-field discipline problems started before the first kickoff and carried throughout the year.

The 2007 season took a nosedive after the Tennessee game with Alabama losing the last four games of the regular season, including a low point loss to Louisiana-Monroe. The Crimson Tide completed the regular season with a 6-6 record and landed a bid to the Independence Bowl in Shreveport, La.

That bowl, however, marked a turning point. Saban would later note that he saw signs of the entire roster beginning to buy into his system during practices before the game, and Alabama defeated Colorado 30-24 to salvage a winning record.

Little did anyone know at the time that the game would mark the start of a 13-game winning streak that would take Alabama back into national championship contention and mark the Crimson Tide's return to glory. ■

Above: Alabama coach Nick Saban runs the media gauntlet at the 2007 SEC Media Days in Hoover. *The Tuscaloosa News | Dusty Compton*
Left: University of Alabama Athletics Director Mal Moore, right, introduces Nick Saban as the new head football coach at a press conference on Jan. 4, 2007. *The Tuscaloosa News | Robert Sutton*

No one predicted an undefeated regular season for the Alabama Crimson Tide in 2008. No expert proclaimed Alabama as a national title contender, a team that would roll through 12 straight opponents and rise to a No. 1 ranking.

For that matter, few expected the Crimson Tide to even contend for the Southeastern Conference Western Division title, much less win it outright and play in the SEC Championship Game. Even the rosiest of forecasts didn't have Alabama playing Florida in the Georgia Dome with not only the SEC title, but also a berth in the BCS Championship Game, on the line.

Yet all of that came to pass, and more.

For the record, Alabama was picked to finish third in its division in the annual preseason poll at SEC Media Days. Three teams received first-place votes in the SEC West, and Alabama wasn't one of them.

Many prognosticators figured the Crimson Tide might be better than it was the year before, but that a tougher schedule would mean little improvement in the won-loss record.

The turning point may have come at the Independence Bowl at the end of the 2007 season, when players

Above: Nick Saban does a walk-through as the team runs drills at a preseason practice.
The Tuscaloosa News | Michael E. Palmer

Top right: Saban watches the team practice.
The Tuscaloosa News | Michael E. Palmer

Right: Linemen run blocking drills during practice.
The Tuscaloosa News | Michael E. Palmer

Top and bottom left: The team runs drills during preseason practice in August. *The Tuscaloosa News | Michael E. Palmer*

Above: Saban leads the team onto the field for the home opener against Tulane. *The Tuscaloosa News | Jasoon Harless*

began to buy into head coach Nick Saban's system, but it got a boost when Saban and his staff landed the nation's top-ranked recruiting class in February, 2008. Difference-makers like Julio Jones, Terrence Cody and Mark Ingram were added to a mix of veterans that included All-America lineman Andre Smith and Antoine Caldwell, a veteran quarterback in John Parker Wilson, a seasoned safety in Rashad Johnson and a ferocious linebacker, Rolando McClain.

Saban also brought in a new offensive coordinator, Jim McElwain, to tutor Wilson, and assistant coach Bobby Williams to improve special teams play.

Most importantly, the Alabama team pulled together.

"I think everybody on this team really cares and respects each other, and that's sort of the intangibles that have made this team play together," Saban would say by season's end.

While many outside the program were skeptical, Alabama players – even before the season's first snap – felt like something special was about to happen.

"Everybody is doing things the right way," Smith said on the first day of practice, "not just some guys doing things the right way. Everybody is buying into Coach Saban's system."

Wilson agreed: "We think we can do some things this year."

Before long, the Alabama Crimson Tide would indeed start to do those things, and surprise the experts. ■

OPPONENT:

CLEMSON

FINAL SCORE: ALABAMA 34 | CLEMSON 10

ATLANTA

It wasn't the vaunted freshmen who made the difference in the University of Alabama's 34-10 win over Clemson at the Georgia Dome in Atlanta. It was the men up front.

The Crimson Tide started pushing Clemson around almost immediately after the opening kickoff and didn't let up. No. 24 Alabama dominated the line of scrimmage on both sides of the ball, running effectively and eradicating the vaunted running game of the No. 9-ranked Tigers, who came into the game as the preseason Atlantic Coast Conference favorite and a dark horse national championship contender.

Instead, it was Alabama that established itself as a team ready to work its way into the national title picture.

"We talked in the off-season about everybody putting themselves in a position physically to play the game," Crimson Tide head coach Nick Saban said. "I'm really pleased and proud of our players.

"We thought the key to the game was not letting them run the ball and running it on offense. We shrunk the game and kept them off the field.

"Skill guys to skill guys (in a matchup), they have very good skill guys. But the key for us was the offensive line and the defensive front."

For Saban, the result was a familiar one.

"This is my fourth time playing here (at the Georgia Dome) and every game has been exactly like that," Saban said. "I've liked every one of them, because we've won them all."

"I cannot remember us getting physically beaten that badly in the last three years," said a forlorn Tiger coach Tommy Bowden, who would resign his position midway through the season. "We created no momentum. We did nothing offensively or defensively to do that.

"We're obviously not the ninth rated team in America."

What became obvious was that Alabama had been seriously underestimated by preseason prognosticators.

The statistical domination was complete. Alabama outgained Clemson 419 yards to 188. The Tigers did not score an offensive touchdown. Clemson finished with zero net yards rushing.

The Crimson Tide was in command for the entire first half, controlling the ball for more than two-thirds of the half and stifling the Clemson offense almost completely.

Leigh Tiffin had three field goals, including a 54-yarder in the first quarter, a new personal best for the Crimson Tide's junior kicker.

A 21-yard Tiffin field goal pushed the Tide lead to 6-0 later in the quarter. The Alabama offensive line took

Left: Coach Nick Saban leads his team onto the field for the second half against Clemson on Aug. 30, 2008. *The Tuscaloosa News | Robert Sutton*

command at that point, with Alabama going on two long touchdown drives.

John Parker Wilson scored on a quarterback sneak for the first Crimson Tide touchdown and a 13-0 lead with 2:51 remaining in the first quarter.

Clemson's only highlight play of the first half, a 47-yard slant pass from Cullen Harper to Jacoby Ford, set up a field goal to make it 13-3.

But throughout the half, Clemson's star running back tandem of James Davis and C.J. Spiller were harder to locate than Osama Bin Laden, vanishing from the Tiger offense.

Dominant on both sides of the line of scrimmage, UA tacked on 10 more points. Wilson capped an 87-yard touchdown march with a 4-yard

Above: Quarterback John Parker Wilson (14) delivers a pass down field as tackle Andre Smith (71) provides protection during first-quarter action against Clemson. *The Tuscaloosa News | Jason Harless*

Left: Punt returner Javier Arenas (28) is tackled by Clemson defender Josh Miller (47) during the first half. *The Tuscaloosa News | Jason Harless*

Far left: Running back Glen Coffee attempts to escape the grasp of a Clemson defender during the first quarter. *The Tuscaloosa News | Jason Harless*

Above: Glen Coffee (38) carries the ball in the first quarter against Clemson.
The Tuscaloosa News | Robert Sutton

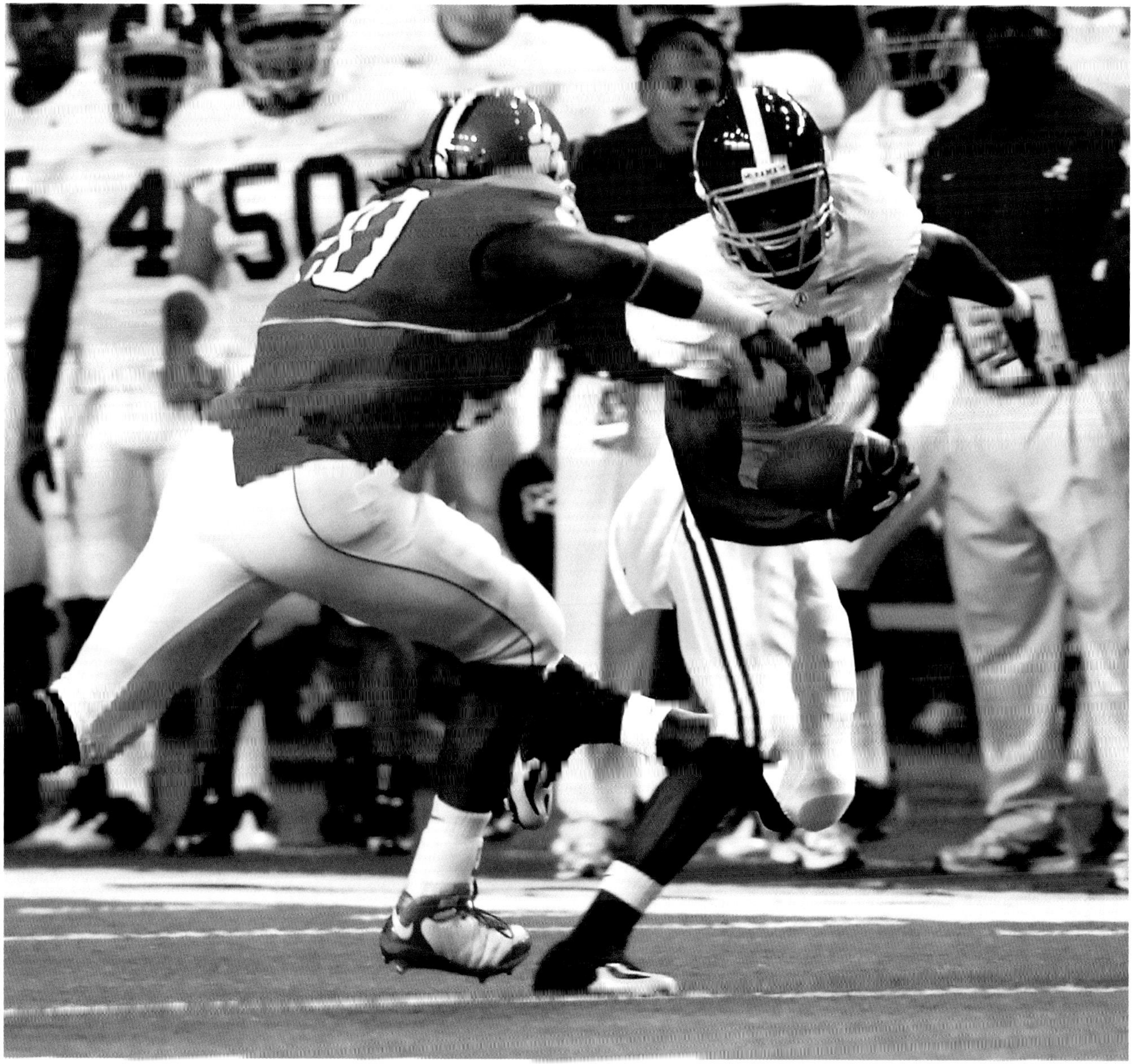

Above: Freshman receiver Julio Jones (8) attempts to elude Clemson defender Brandon Maye (20)after making a reception during the first quarter. *The Tuscaloosa News | Jason Harless*

Top right: Coach Nick Saban applauds the team during the first quarter. *The Tuscaloosa News | Robert Sutton*

Right: Alabama freshman Mark Ingram (22) carries the ball. *The Tuscaloosa News | Robert Sutton*

Opposite page: Ingram celebrates his two-point conversion in the third quarter. *The Tuscaloosa News | Robert Sutton*

Above: Quarterback John Parker Wilson (14) looks for a receiver. *The Tuscaloosa News | Robert Sutton*

Opposite page left: Antoine Caldwell celebrates in the final seconds of Alabama's victory over Clemson. *The Tuscaloosa News | Jason Harless*

Opposite page right: Alabama head coach Nick Saban talks with Clemson head coach Tommy Bowden prior to the opener in the Georgia Dome. *The Tuscaloosa News | Jason Harless*

GAME STATS

UA VS. CLEMSON | AUG. 30, 2008

Score by quarters	1	2	3	4	Final
Alabama	13	10	8	3	34
Clemson	0	3	7	0	10

Team statistics	Ala.	Clem.
First downs	25	11
— By rush	13	2
— By pass	10	8
— By penalty	2	1
Rushing attempts	50	14
Yds. gained rushing	247	30
Yds. lost rushing	8	30
Net yds. rushing	239	0
Passes attempted	30	34
Passes completed	22	20
Had intercepted	0	1
Net yds. passing	180	188
Total offensive plays	80	48
Total offense	419	188
Avg. gain per play	5.2	3.9
Fumbles-lost	0-0	1-1
Interceptions-yds.	1-7	0-0
Penalties-yds.	6-40	6-43
Punts-yards	2-73	4-160
Yards per punt	36.5	40.0
Punt returns-yds.	2-23	1-9
Kickoff returns-yds.	3-61	7-188
Possession	41:13	18:47
3rd-down conv.	11-17	1-9

AP Top 25

1. Georgia (0-0)
2. Ohio State (0-0)
3. Southern Cal (0-0)
4. Oklahoma (0-0)
5. Florida (0-0)
6. Missouri (0-0)
7. LSU (0-0)
8. West Virginia (0-0)
9. Clemson (0-0)
10. Auburn (0-0)
11. Texas (0-0)
12. Texas Teach (0-0)
13. Wisconsin (0-0)
14. Kansas (0-0)
15. Arizona State (0-0)
16. BYU (0-0)
17. Virginia Tech (0-0)
18. Tennessee (0-0)
19. South Florida (0-0)
20. Illinois (0-0)
21. Oregon (0-0)
22. Penn State (0-0)
23. Wake Forest (0-0)
24. **Alabama (0-0)**
25. Pittsburgh (0-0)

touchdown pass to tight end Nick Walker. Marquis Johnson's interception with 1:39 left in the half ended a Clemson drive in Tide territory, and Alabama marched back to set up Tiffin's third field goal, a 34-yarder, as time expired in the half.

Spiller did assert himself on special teams as the second half began, taking the kickoff 96 yards for a touchdown that cut Alabama's lead to 23-10. But things quickly resumed the familiar pattern — Alabama imposing its will and Clemson finding itself unable to do much about it.

The Crimson Tide scored on a 67-yard march later in the quarter, with Wilson completing a 4-yard touchdown pass to Julio Jones for the score, the first signal of an outstanding year to come from the freshman wide receiver. Another heralded rookie, running back Mark Ingram, added a two-point conversion as icing.

The major concern on that drive, and one of the few dark clouds of the evening, was the status of Alabama's All-America left tackle, Andre Smith. The junior had to be helped from the field with a knee injury and did not return to the game, although he remained on the sidelines.

Clemson was probably clinically beyond revival at that point, but the final punctuation came when the Tigers turned the ball over on downs at the Alabama 11 with 12:33 to play.

The Crimson Tide tacked on one more field goal by Tiffin for the final margin.

Wilson was efficient, completing 22 of 30 passes for 180 yards, two touchdowns and no interceptions. Walker had seven catches for 67 yards. ■

TULANE
TULANE
TULANE

OPPONENT:

TULANE

FINAL SCORE: ALABAMA 20 | TULANE 6

The University of Alabama's hopes for a dream football season didn't come crashing down in a game that left many Crimson Tide supporters scratching their heads, but those dreams seemed to have gotten a little bruised.

No. 13-ranked Alabama, fresh off a demolition of Clemson in its previous game, struggled all night before finishing off Tulane, 20-6.

"It's great to win, but it's not always great to win when you don't feel like you played relative to your capabilities," Crimson Tide head coach Nick Saban said after the game. "I certainly don't think we did that tonight. It's a little disappointing.

"The goal was to play with consistency, to come out and show who we are. We weren't able to do that."

Saban said that special-teams play and defense were the difference in the game.

"The defense didn't always play great," he said. "We had a couple of big plays, a couple of penalties, that hurt us. We didn't get off the field on third down as much as we needed to, but we kept them out of end zone and that was a key to the game.

"The players we had in there are capable of playing well enough that we should have been able to move the ball and do some good things. We had three offensive linemen playing in different places than they usually play, but we should have the personnel to do better."

All-American left tackle Andre Smith was out with a sprained knee, and guard Marlon Davis had to leave with a strained hamstring. Saban said he was "hopeful" that both would be back in the lineup in the coming days.

Saban also said that the excitement that followed the Clemson game presented a psychological obstacle for the Crimson Tide. He

Above: Chris Rogers (8) picks up a blocked punt and runs it in for a touchdown in the second quarter. *The Tuscaloosa News | Dusty Compton*

Left: Kareem Jackson (3) picks up a Tulane third-quarter fumble. *The Tuscaloosa News | Dusty Compton*

issued strong warnings almost as soon as the Clemson game was over that Alabama couldn't rest on its laurels just because of one impressive victory.

"Obviously, (last week) had an effect on our team," he said. "I've been criticized for trying to talk about things we need to focus on, but you've got to think about the right stuff (as a team). We'll get better because of this. Everyone needs to do a better job, including me."

The Crimson Tide, working with a patchwork offensive line that did not include either Smith at tackle or Davis at guard, struggled mightily in the first half.

Had it not been for the Crimson Tide's punt-return team, the scoreboard might have more closely reflected those problems. But the Crimson Tide made two big plays in the special-teams phase of the game to build a lead.

Javier Arenas had the first of those plays, an 87-yard punt return with just over 10 minutes remaining in the first quarter that gave UA a 7-0 lead. Arenas returned three more punts before halftime and broke Harry Gilmer's six-decade-old school record for return yards in a game before 30 minutes had even ticked off the clock.

Arenas finished the half with 141 yards on four punt returns. In addition to the touchdown, he twice set the Crimson Tide offense up in Tulane territory, only to see offensive misfires squander the field position.

"He has a unique knack to make big plays and to make people miss him in space," Saban said of Arenas.

The second Alabama touchdown also came on a punt return of sorts, this time of the blocked variety. Roy Upchurch blocked Darren deRochemont's kick at the Tulane 17, and Chris Rogers scooped it up for an easy score.

There was nothing else easy about the first half for UA. Alabama finished with just 38 yards of total offense. The net rushing total was zero yards, due to four sacks of John Parker Wilson that resulted in 29 yards in losses.

There was some improvement in the second half, although it was not vast. Alabama did generate the game's only sustained touchdown march in the latter part of the third quarter, covering 77 yards on 11 plays for a touchdown that gave UA a comfortable 20-3 lead. Freshman Mark Ingram had the score on a 15-yard run as time expired in the third quarter.

Above: Alabama's record-setting punt returner Javier Arenas (28) moves the ball upfield while being pursued by a host of Tulane defenders during a second-quarter kick return.
The Tuscaloosa News | Dusty Compton

Left: Alabama running back Mark Ingram (22) makes his way downfield during a third-quarter drive.
The Tuscaloosa News | Dusty Compton

GAME STATS

UA VS. TULANE | SEPT. 6, 2008

SCORE BY QUARTERS	1	2	3	4	FINAL
Tulane	[illegible]	[illegible]	[illegible]	[illegible]	[illegible]
Alabama	[illegible]	[illegible]	[illegible]	[illegible]	20

Team statistics	Tul.	Ala.
First downs	18	11
— By rush	6	4
— By pass	11	6
— By penalty	1	1
Rushing attempts	32	26
Yds. gained rushing	101	130
Yds. lost rushing	15	31
Net yds. rushing	86	99
Passes attempted	50	23
Passes completed	29	11
Had intercepted	0	0
Net yds. passing	232	73
Total offensive plays	82	49
Total offense	318	172
Avg. gain per play	3.9	3.5
Fumbles-lost	2-0	1-1
Interceptions-yds.	0-0	0-0
Penalties-yds.	4-29	6-43
Punts yards	7-226	7-280
Yards per punt	32.3	40.0
Punt returns-yds.	2-8	7-171
Kickoff returns-yds.	3-46	3-91
Possession	36:35	23:25
3rd-down conv.	7-20	3-11

AP Top 25

1. USC (1-0)
2. Georgia (1-0)
3. Ohio State (1-0)
4. Oklahoma (1-0)
5. Florida (1-0)
6. Missouri (1-0)
7. LSU (1-0)
8. West Virginia (1-0)
9. Auburn (1-0)
10. Texas (1-0)
11. Wisconsin (1-0)
12. Texas Tech (1-0)
13. **Alabama (1-0)**
14. Kansas (1-0)
15. Arizona State (1-0)
16. Brigham Young (1-0)
17. South Florida (1-0)
18. Oregon (1-0)
19. Penn State (1-0)
20. Wake Forest (1-0)
21. Fresno State (1-0)
22. Utah (1-0)
23. UCLA (1-0)
24. Illinois (0-1)
24. South Carolina (1-0)

Above: Alabama's Marquis Maze (4) is pulled down by Tulane's Corey Sonnier (38) on a third-quarter reception.
The Tuscaloosa News | [illegible]

Above left: [illegible] (30) carries the ball in the first half.
The Tuscaloosa News | Robert Sutton

Left: Tyrone King ([illegible]) and Ali Sharrief (28) celebrate with Chris Rogers (8).
The Tuscaloosa News | Robert Sutton

Tulane added a 21-yard Ross Thevenot field goal, his second of the game, in the fourth quarter, but could pull no closer.

The Green Wave outgained Alabama, 316 yards to 172. That discrepancy was balanced somewhat by Alabama's 202-55 edge in kick-return yardage, but still didn't reflect well on the offensive effort. The Tide's time of possession, which exceeded 40 minutes in the win over Clemson, was just a shade over 23 minutes against Tulane.

Kevin Moore, the Green Wave quarterback, threw 49 passes, completing 28 for a total of 225 yards. ■

OPPONENT: WESTERN KENTUCKY

FINAL SCORE: ALABAMA 41 | WESTERN KENTUCKY 7

What was essentially the final dress rehearsal for the University of Alabama football team before the curtain went up on the Southeastern Conference season went as well as Nick Saban had hoped, with only a few flubbed lines and plenty of chances for every actor to get on the stage, at least for a little while.

The Crimson Tide took control early and rolled up 557 total yards en route to a 41-7 dismantling of Western Kentucky at Bryant-Denny Stadium.

"We really did play like we wanted to play last week and this week," Saban said. "We started with a three and out on defense, then got the ball and had an 11-play drive for a touchdown. So we started the game out well.

"But more importantly, we finished."

The theme Saban would sound throughout the season was on full display as Alabama, indeed, finished what it started against the Hilltoppers.

The Crimson Tide had a 31-7 lead at halftime, then scored 10 points in the first 10 minutes of the third quarter, allowing the coaches to use the final 20 minutes as a forum for free substitution. A total of 67 players saw action for UA, by far the most to this point of the season.

"The goal in this game (for our players) was to go prove you could play to your capacity, to play your best football because of competitive capacity you have," Saban said. "We wanted to go out, try to dominate competitively, and we did that.

"We got to play a lot of players," he added. "We were real pleased with that. Now we can look at (those players) and make some evaluations."

The Crimson Tide was well balanced on offense, running for 281 yards and passing for 276 more.

Six different Alabama rushers ran for 20 yards or more in the game.

Left: Alabama defenders Brandon Fanney (98) and Rolando McClain, right, bring down a Western Kentucky player during the first quarter. *The Tuscaloosa News | Dan Lopez*

Above: Alabama receiver Nikita Stover (9) is tackled during the first quarter. *The Tuscaloosa News | Dan Lopez*

Glen Coffee had 11 carries for a game-high 98 yards, and Mark Ingram added two touchdown runs on his nine carries, even though neither Coffee nor Ingram touched the ball in the second half.

"That is something we always strive for, to be able to run the football," Saban said. "We did a really good job of controlling the line of scrimmage, and we made some plays in the passing game. We still had some miscues. We need to clean those up, but we made some of those explosive plays we hadn't been making."

John Parker Wilson quarterbacked for the first three quarters, completing 17 of 27 passes for 215 yards and two touchdowns. Wilson upped his total to 41 touchdown passes in his career, tying Brodie Croyle's school record.

"John Parker had some struggles last week, but I don't think the people around him played well," Saban said. "He has done a really good job for us all year. He did throw one interception tonight, when they dropped deep and he should have gone to the check-down. But we're making progress."

Alabama took a 17-0 lead in the first quarter on two Ingram touch-

Top left: Quarterback Greg McElroy throws under pressure in front of Western Kentucky defenders in the fourth quarter. *The Tuscaloosa News | Dan Lopez*

Above : Coach Nick Saban reacts after Western Kentucky returns an Alabama kickoff 32 yards during the first half. *The Tuscaloosa News | Jason Harless*

Left: Alabama's Julio Jones (8) comes down with a reception as a Western Kentucky defender makes the tackle during the first half. *The Tuscaloosa News | Jason Harless*

GAME STATS

UA VS. W. KENTUCKY | SEPT. 13, 2008

Score by quarters	1	2	3	4	Final
W. Kentucky	0	7	0	0	7
Alabama	17	14	10	0	41

Team statistics	W.K.	Ala.
First downs	9	30
— By rush	2	16
— By pass	6	14
— By penalty	1	0
Rushing attempts	22	49
Yds. gained rushing	68	294
Yds. lost rushing	26	13
Net yds. rushing	42	281
Passes attempted	26	33
Passes completed	14	21
Had intercepted	1	1
Net yds. passing	116	276
Total offensive plays	48	82
Total offense	158	557
Avg. gain per play	3.3	6.8
Fumbles-lost	2-1	1-1
Interceptions-yds.	1-18	1-1
Penalties-yds.	5-27	3-25
Punts-yards	7-255	0-0
Yards per punt	36.4	0.0
Punt returns-yds.	0-0	4-53
Kickoff returns-yds.	8-161	1-9
Possession	22:39	37:21
3rd-down conv.	3-12	9-14

AP Top 25

1. USC (1-0)
2. Georgia (2-0)
3. Oklahoma (2-0)
4. Florida (2-0)
5. Ohio State (2-0)
6. Missouri (2-0)
7. LSU (1-0)
8. Texas (2-0)
9. Auburn (2-0)
10. Wisconsin (2-0)
11. **Alabama (2-0)**
12. Texas Tech (2-0)
13. Kansas (2-0)
14. East Carolina (2-0)
15. Arizona State
16. Oregon (2-0)
17. Penn State (2-0)
18. Brigham Young (2-0)
19. South Florida (2-0)
20. Wake Forest (2-0)
21. Fresno State (1-0)
22. Utah (2-0)
23. California (2-0)
24. Illinois (1-1)
25. West Virginia (1-1)

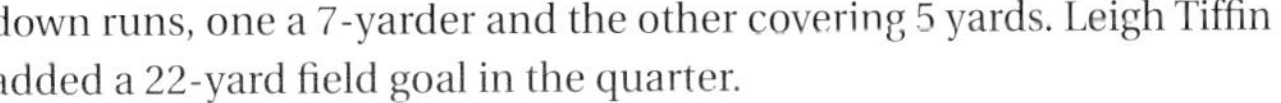

down runs, one a 7-yarder and the other covering 5 yards. Leigh Tiffin added a 22-yard field goal in the quarter.

The Crimson Tide cruised after that, with the only glitch coming in the second quarter.

Western Kentucky did manage the first touchdown against the Alabama defense in more than 140 minutes this season, scoring on a 30-yard pass from David Wolke to Tristan Jones with 4:21 remaining in the first half. That drive had been set up by the lone Wilson interception.

Alabama was already up 24-0 at that point, thanks to Terry Grant's 8-yard touchdown run.

Wilson added his two touchdown passes, a 2-yarder to tight end Nick Walker and a 12-yarder to freshman Julio Jones, as the Tide built its comfortable final margin. ■

Top left: Mark Ingram (22) fights his way across the goal line for a touchdown in the first quarter.
The Tuscaloosa News | Michael E. Palmer
Above: Ingram celebrates after scoring Alabama's first touchdown of the game. *The Tuscaloosa News | Jason Harless*
Left: Alabama noseguard Terrence Cody (62) displays the ball after recovering a Western Kentucky fumble during the first half.
The Tuscaloosa News | Jason Harless

TIME OUT WITH

#62 TERRENCE CODY

When the Alabama football team arrived at the Georgia Dome for its walk-though prior to playing Florida in the SEC Championship Game, the players looked focused and intense, with their game faces already on.

There was one exception, the big guy who was smiling and singing like had been ever since arriving at the Capstone. No one may have been happier to be there than Terrence Cody.

At 6-foot-5 and 365 pounds, the junior-college transfer was the Crimson Tide's version of the missing link, and when he was at his best, no opponent dared try to run up the middle against Alabama.

Clemson was his coming-out party, when the Tigers, despite having arguably the best running back tandem in the nation with C.J. Spiller and James Davis, were statistically held to zero rushing yards.

Tulane and Western Kentucky learned the hard way, too, and before long opponents were trying to attack the defense from the outside in, still with limited success. Even Georgia's Knowshon Moreno, who would win the SEC rushing title, tallied just 34 yards against Cody & Co.

"If I had seen the ball, I probably could have grabbed it and probably run with it," Cody said with a laugh about his fumble recovery after pushing WKU's center back into the ball-carrier. "I just fell on it

because that's what I was told to do."

Though limited by a knee sprain later in the season, Cody certainly left his mark and became an instant cult hero on campus — long before he lined up at fullback for true freshman Mark Ingram's 2-yard touchdown plunge against Ole Miss. When Cody was in the backfield against Auburn, nobody in white wanted anything to do with him.

"He's a big load in there," said Arkansas coach Bobby Petrino, who helplessly watched Cody lead a goal-line stand against his Razorbacks.

Facing senior center Antoine Caldwell every day in practice contributed to his development, as Cody improved his conditioning and got under 400 pounds. Caldwell, a first-team All-America center, admitted Cody was almost impossible to block single-handedly, especially since he's quick off the snap and is surprisingly fast for his size.

"That's helped me out a lot," Cody said. "It's made me smarter on the line, made me quicker off the ball trying to anticipate what he's going to do."

Cody wasn't just unique for the Crimson Tide, but college football as a whole. So when the nickname was finally uttered, it stuck, Mr. Cody

"All-American, all-globe, I don't care what they are," junior cornerback Javier Arenas said about watching opponents try to deal with Cody. "It's fascinating to watch them get pushed back because they're huge, but this huger guy is putting them in the quarterback's lap." ■

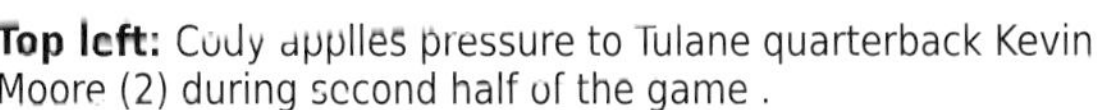

Top left: Cody applies pressure to Tulane quarterback Kevin Moore (2) during second half of the game .
The Tuscaloosa News | Dusty Compton
Above: Cody falls on a Western Kentucky fumble in the first quarter. *The Tuscaloosa News | Michael E. Palmer*
Opposite page: Cody works with the team during practice. *The Tuscaloosa News | Michael E. Palmer*

SEC
BAMA
ARKANSAS
HOGS

OPPONENT:

ARKANSAS

FINAL SCORE: ALABAMA 49 | ARKANSAS 14

The fog burned off early at Razorback Stadium. That left thunder and lightning.

The thunder was provided by the University of Alabama offensive and defensive lines, who dominated the Razorbacks all day long. The lightning came from a steady supplement of long touchdowns — six covering 25 yards or more and four of those going for more than 60 yards — as Alabama buried Arkansas 49-14 in the Southeastern Conference opener for both teams.

It was Alabama's most one-sided SEC road win since a 62-27 beatdown of Ole Miss in Jackson, Miss., in 1989. The 49 points were the most Alabama had scored in any SEC game, home or away, since it put 59 points up against Vanderbilt in 1990. It was the first time since 1993 that Alabama had scored 40 or more points in back-to-back games.

Alabama did it despite some occasional lapses, especially on defense.

"We probably made more mental mistakes in this game than we have all year," said Crimson Tide head coach Nick Saban. "But we did a great job at the line of scrimmage. That's how we were able to overcome."

"That's a tough game for us," said Arkansas' first-year coach Bobby Petrino. "We've got to get to the point where we don't beat ourselves, and we've got a long way to go."

It only required one early Arkansas mistake, a penalty for running into the kicker, to open the floodgates — although the deluge was likely to come sooner or later. That penalty did prolong

Far left: Alabama's Marquis Maze (4) is knocked out of bounds by an Arkansas defender on a fourth-quarter punt return. *The Tuscaloosa News | Dusty Compton*

Left: Justin Woodall (27) carries an interception across the goal line for a 74-yard touchdown in the second quarter. *The Tuscaloosa News | Dusty Compton*

Alabama's first drive, which culminated in 1-yard touchdown run by Mark Ingram.

The Tide's next possession was more electric, if far shorter.

Glen Coffee took a handoff and went untouched for an 87-yard touchdown.

Alabama added three more touchdowns in the half, two on long interception returns of ill-advised Casey Dick throws.

Javier Arenas had a 63-yard interception return with 53 seconds remaining in the first quarter. Justin Woodall eclipsed that in the second quarter, picking off a Dick pass and going 74 yards for the score. That was Alabama's longest touchdown interception return since Reggie Myles returned one for a 91-yard score against UCLA in 2000.

The two defensive scores sandwiched a pass from John Parker Wilson to Julio Jones for a 25-yard touchdown.

Arkansas did manage to convert on fourth down for a 12-yard touchdown pass from Dick to Andrew Davis in the second quarter.

On its other foray deep into Crimson Tide territory, the Razorbacks were stuffed on four downs from the Crimson Tide 2 as the first half ticked away. That stand supplied the punctuation mark for the Hogs' misery.

"We were reeling a little on defense at that point," Saban said.

"We had made a lot of mental errors on that drive. Our players were tired. The defense played a lot of plays in the first half. So for (Arkansas) to get the ball to the 1-yard line and for us to stop them, that said a lot. It was all things we practice every day. We just had to go and execute them, but it said a lot about the competitive character of our team."

The second half was more or less an exercise

Above: Alabama reciever Marquis Maze (4) looks for yardage against Arkansas in the fourth quarter.
The Tuscaloosa News | Michael E. Palmer

Top left: Quarterback John Parker Wilson throws a pass in the third quarter.
The Tuscaloosa News | Michael E. Palmer

Left: Coach Nick Saban offers encouragement to his players at the start of the game.
The Tuscaloosa News | Michael E. Palmer

WASHINGTON

Below: Javier Arenas (28) evades Arkansas quarterback Casey Dick for a touchdown after an interception in the first quarter. *The Tuscaloosa News | Dusty Compton*
Right: Quarterback John Parker Wilson (14) gets sacked by two Arkansas defenders in the third quarter. *The Tuscaloosa News | Michael E. Palmer*

in mutual clock killing, although Alabama did add two more explosive touchdowns on a 31-yard run by Coffee and a 62-yarder by Roy Upchurch.

Arkansas added one consolation touchdown directed by backup quarterback Tyler Wilson.

"I was very pleased and proud with the way we played," Saban said. "I don't want people to think otherwise. But we still have some things we can improve on."

Coffee paced the offense, rushing for 162 yards on 10 carries. That set a new school record for yards per attempt with a minimum of 10 carries. Coffee's 16.2 yards per carry eclipsed the old mark (14.6 yards per carry) set by Shaun Alexander against LSU in 1996.

As a team, Alabama averaged 9.4 yards per rush. Wilson eclipsed the Tide's career touchdown passing record with his throw to Jones, the 42nd touchdown pass of Wilson's career. He threw just 14 times, completing six for 74 yards, but noted that Alabama's big early lead made passing superfluous.

"When we're up like that, we are not going to throw every down," he said. "With the way we were running and the way our defense was playing, we weren't about to mess anything up. We were just going to pound the ball." ■

Above: Glen Coffee (38) is pursued by an Arkansas defender on an 87-yard touchdown run in the first quarter. *The Tuscaloosa News | Dusty Compton*

Left: Coffee is embraced by Mike McCoy after completing the 87-yard touchdown play. *The Tuscaloosa News | Dusty Compton*

GAME STATS

UA VS. ARKANSAS | SEPT. 12, 2008

Score by quarters	1	2	3	4	Final
Alabama	21	14	7	7	49
Arkansas	0	7	0	7	14

Team statistics	Ala.	Ark
First downs	15	19
— By rush	11	7
— By pass	3	12
— By penalty	1	0
Rushing attempts	35	31
Yds. gained rushing	343	115
Yds. lost rushing	15	23
Net yds. rushing	328	92
Passes attempted	15	46
Passes completed	6	24
Had intercepted	1	4
Net yds. passing	74	217
Total offensive plays	50	77
Total offense	402	309
Avg. gain per play	8.0	4.0
Fumbles-lost	2-0	2-0
Interceptions-yds.	4-131	1-0
Penalties-yds	1-10	5-30
Punts-yards	5-226	7-304
Yards per punt	45.2	37.7
Punt returns-yds.	5-20	3-20
Kickoff returns-yds.	3-34	8-184
Possession	25:14	34:46
3rd-down conv.	4-11	5-17

AP Top 25

1. USC (2-0)
2. Oklahoma (3-0)
3. Georgia (3-0)
4. Florida (2-0)
5. Missouri (3-0)
6. LSU (2-0)
7. Texas (2-0)
8. Wisconsin (3-0)
9. **Alabama (3-0)**
10. Auburn (3-0)
11. Texas Tech (3-0)
12. South Florida (3-0)
13. Ohio State (2-1)
14. Brigham Young (3-0)
15. East Carolina (3-0)
16. Penn State (3-0)
17. Oregon (3-0)
18. Wake Forest (2-0)
19. Kansas (2-1)
20. Utah (3-0)
21. West Virginia (1-1)
22. Illinois (2-1)
23. Clemson (2-1)
24. Florida State (2-0)
25. Fresno State (1-1)

38
COFFEE

OPPONENT:

GEORGIA

FINAL SCORE: ALABAMA 41 | GEORGIA 30

A blackout?

A wipeout was more like it.

The University of Alabama rolled to a 31-point halftime lead, then did enough in the second half to seal the tomb on the black-clad Bulldogs, shaking up the Southeastern Conference and perhaps the nation with a 41-30 victory over the Bulldogs at Sanford Stadium in Athens.

Georgia didn't go quietly after falling behind 31-0 at the half, taking advantage of Crimson Tide foibles in the kicking game — a blocked punt, a 92-yard punt return and an onside kick recovery — and some solid passing by Matthew Stafford to make the score respectable, if not more palatable for the third-ranked Bulldogs.

Alabama's impressive victory came over a team ranked No. 1 in the nation in the preseason. Georgia fans, players and coaches wore black in keeping with the school's "blackout" theme for the game.

In the end, the black may as well have been worn in mourning.

"I'm happy," said Alabama coach Nick Saban.

"This is a great win for us. Georgia has a great program and a great team. We probably played the best half of football we've played all season long, and it couldn't have come at a better time."

The 41 points were the most Alabama has ever scored against a Georgia team in the 65-game history of the series. It marked the first

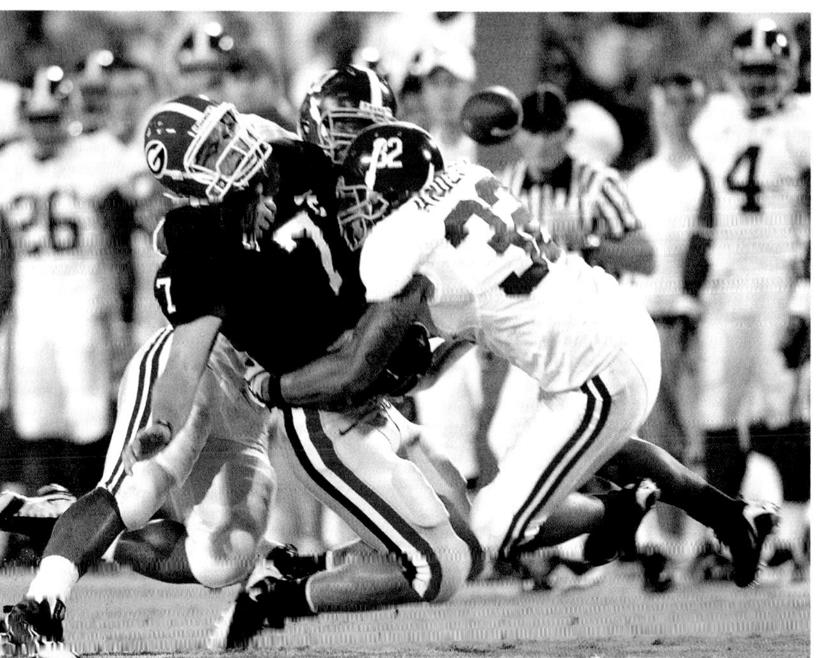

Above: Alabama defenders Eryk Anders (32) and Lorenzo Washington (97) bring down Georgia quarterback Matthew Stafford during the second quarter. *The Tuscaloosa News | Jason Harless*

Left: Glen Coffee (38) drives over the goal line for a touchdown in the second quarter. *The Tuscaloosa News | Dusty Compton*

time since the 1979 national championship team that Alabama had scored 40 points in back-to-back SEC road games.

The first half was a Bulldog nightmare from the beginning.

Two crucial Georgia penalties — a pass interference call and a personal foul — aided the first Crimson Tide drive, giving Alabama 27 yards and negating an Alabama fumble.

Alabama also did plenty of work on its own, including two catches by Julio Jones. Fellow freshman Mark Ingram capped the march with a 6-yard touchdown run.

Georgia continued to transgress on the next Crimson Tide drive, committing two more major fouls to maintain a UA drive that ended with a 23-yard Leigh Tiffin field goal.

That kick gave the Tide a 10-0 lead with 49 seconds remaining in the first quarter.

The second quarter will go down in Alabama history, a 21-point explosion that essentially settled the game, despite Georgia's second-half gallantry.

An 18-yard Georgia punt set up a 48-yard march for the next Crimson Tide score. A 32-yard completion from John Parker Wilson to Jones set up the score, a 3-yard run by Glenn Coffee.

On the next Georgia possession, Alabama linebacker Dont'a Hightower grabbed a football that was bobbled by Bulldog receiver A.J. Green.

The turnover put Alabama back in business at the Georgia 33, the starting point for a seven-play march. Roy Upchurch scored on a 4-yard run to put Alabama ahead 24-0 with 6:47 remaining.

The Crimson Tide capped one of the greatest first halves

Above: Alabama's Roy Upchurch (5) leaps over Georgias defenders for a second-quarter touchdown.
The Tuscaloosa News | Dusty Compton

Top left: Javier Arenas is tackled in the first quarter.
The Tuscaloosa News | Robert Sutton

Left: Disappointed Georgia students and fans react during the game.
The Tuscaloosa News | Jason Harless

Opposite page: Alabama receiver Julio Jones (8) brings in a 23-yard pass for an Alabama touchdown.
The Tuscaloosa News | Jason Harless

Top left: John Parker Wilson throws the ball to a receiver in the second quarter.
The Tuscaloosa News | Dusty Compton

Above: Roy Upchurch is knocked off his feet by a Georgia defender in the fourth quarter.
The Tuscaloosa News | Dusty Compton

Far left: John Parker Wilson attempts to elude a Georgia defensive lineman after being flushed from the pocket.
The Tuscaloosa News | Jason Harless

Left: Roy Upchurch carries the ball in the fourth quarter against the Bulldogs.
The Tuscaloosa News | Robert Sutton

INSIDE THE GAME

The Alabama Crimson Tide flexed its defensive muscle in the first half against No. 3 Georgia, shutting the Bulldogs out while holding them to four first downs and just 86 yards.

Alabama relaxed its grip in the second half, allowing the Bulldogs to roll up 238 yards and pile up 16 first downs in the third and fourth quarters.

So what was the difference?

"We were way more intense in the first half," cornerback Javier Arenas said. "In the second half we had position on them and we had a lead. We were up so much we made them pass."

Alabama also made Georgia's all-star running back, Knowshon Moreno, a non-factor. The Bulldogs gained 15 yards on a pass play on their first offensive snap and threw a screen pass to Moreno for 13 more yards on the next play, but gained just four yards the rest of the first quarter.

For the game, Moreno ran for just 34 yards on nine attempts with a touchdown, his worst outing on the way to second-team All-America honors.

"We said that it was really, really important that we not have to play an eight-man front to stop their run, and for the most part we did that," Alabama head coach Nick Saban said.

After Moreno's big gainer on the first pass, the Tide was able to take him out of Georgia's screen-heavy passing game. He caught two more passes for one net yard.

"We just had to realize when he was trying to step up and slip by you," UA linebacker Cory Reamer said. "They were trying to slip him out, and we used a lot of different people to cover him."

Georgia quarterback Matthew Stafford lit Alabama up for 274 yards and two touchdowns on 24-of-42 passing, but he also threw his first interception of the season when Justin Woodall picked off a long pass at the end of the first half.

The Tide got another turnover out of Georgia's passing game when Dont'a Hightower recovered a fumble by receiver A.J. Green earlier in the second quarter.

Stafford tallied just 63 passing yards in the first half. Georgia had to all but abandon the run after trailing 31-0 at halftime, and Stafford's big arm began to produce in the third quarter.

"We had good coverage on several guys and couldn't make the play, or didn't make the play," Saban said.

Reamer said the UA defense was more effective in the first half because the players did what they were told and played at full intensity.

"The second half we slipped up a little bit," he said. ■

Above: Mark Ingram (22) runs inside the 10-yard line as Georgia defenders attempt to make the tackle during the first quarter.
The Tuscaloosa News | Jason Harless

Right: Ingram (22) carries the ball for a touchdown in the first quarter.
The Tuscaloosa News | Robert Sutton

GAME STATS

UA VS. GEORGIA | SEPT. 27, 2008

Score by quarters	1	2	3	4	Final
Alabama	10	21	0	10	41
Georgia	0	0	10	20	30

Team statistics	Ala.	UGA
First downs	21	18
—By rush	6	2
—By pass	11	15
—By penalty	4	1
Rushing attempts	45	16
Yds. gained rushing	145	68
Yds. lost rushing	16	18
Net yds. rushing	129	50
Passes attempted	16	43
Passes completed	13	24
Had intercepted	0	1
Net yds. passing	205	274
Total offensive plays	61	59
Total offense	334	324
Avg. gain per play	5.5	5.5
Fumbles-lost	2-1	1-1
Interceptions-yds.	1-12	0-0
Penalties-yds.	2-9	10-91
Punts-yards	3-102	4-121
Yards per punt	34.0	30.2
Punt returns-yds.	2-27	1-92
Kickoff returns-yds.	8-517	5-287
Possession	35:46	24:14
3rd-down conv.	4-10	4-13

AP Top 25

1. USC (2-0)
2. Oklahoma (3-0)
3. Georgia (4-0)
4. Florida (3-0)
5. LSU (3-0)
6. Missouri (4-0)
7. Texas (3-0)
8. **Alabama (4-0)**
9. Wisconsin (3-0)
10. Texas Tech (4-0)
11. Brigham Young (4-0)
12. Penn State (4-0)
13. South Florida (4-0)
14. Ohio State (3-1)
15. Auburn (3-1)
16. Wake Forest (3-0)
17. Utah (4-0)
18. Kansas (3-1)
19. Boise State (3-0)
20. Clemson (3-1)
21. Vanderbilt (4-0)
22. Illinois (2-1)
23. East Carolina (3-1)
24. TCU (4-0)
25. Fresno State (2-1)

Left: Roy Upchurch (5) is congratulated by guard Mike Johnson (78) after a second-quarter touchdown.
The Tuscaloosa News | Dusty Compton

Left: Alabama defensive coordinator Kirby Smart gets a piggyback ride on the back of defensive lineman Terrence Cody after their victory. *The Tuscaloosa News | Jason Harless*
Below: Nick Saban, right, and Georgia head coach Mark Richt meet after the game *The Tuscaloosa News | Dusty Compton*

in its history when Wilson hit Jones with a 22-yard touchdown.

By halftime, it was clear that this Alabama team had played itself into the national picture and was on its way to becoming a serious contender for the national title.

Trailing 31-0, Georgia rallied to make it a two-touchdown game, scoring a field goal and a touchdown (on a Knowshon Moreno run) in the third quarter.

Prince Miller's 92-yard punt return with 14:41 to play suddenly breathed real life into the Bulldogs as they pulled within 14 points at 31-17

Alabama answered with a Leigh Tiffin field goal to make the score 34-17 with 9:45 remaining, then put the game away for good with 4:13 to go when Coffee scored on a 13-yard run.

Stafford threw two touchdown passes in the final three minutes to make the score less lopsided.

With Georgia forced to throw exclusively in the fourth quarter, the Bulldog running game was limited to just 50 yards.

"They definitely stopped our run game," said Georgia coach Mark Richt. "Matthew Stafford wasn't able to get his feet and throw the ball the way we like him to, so that tells me they did a pretty good job up front.

"They just took it to us, and we didn't answer until the second half. We did answer in the second half. We never gave in, but we dug such a deep hole we were never getting out of it." ■

2
NTUCKY
BAMA
BAMA

OPPONENT:

KENTUCKY

FINAL SCORE: ALABAMA 17 | KENTUCKY 14

The University of Alabama football team had all the ingredients for a win that was as easy as a piece of cake — a 200-yard rusher in Glen Coffee, a couple of defensive takeaways and a hungry audience just waiting to enjoy a post-Georgia dessert.

Somehow, the ingredients never quite came together. The Crimson Tide missed some scoring opportunities, allowed a couple of big plays on defense and wound up needing a poorly executed Kentucky onside kick to survive with a 17-14 victory at Bryant-Denny Stadium.

“We're certainly happy with the win,” Crimson Tide head coach Nick Saban said. “But we put on a clinic for how to keep the other team in the game.”

The win did push No. 2-ranked Alabama to 6-0 at the mid-point of the season heading into an open week. The loss was the first for Kentucky after four non-conference wins.

Saban said the Crimson Tide's struggles were not attributable to a lack of intensity.

“We were ahead 14-0 at the half, had 253 yards to their 60, so we must have had something,” Saban said, responding to a question about his team's “lack of energy.”

“The problem in the first half was that we didn't score points to match what we had done. We missed a field goal, we fumbled in the red zone and we left some other plays out there because of penalties.”

Alabama seemed to have finally delivered the knockout punch with a fourth-quarter drive — almost entirely on the ground — that consumed more than eight minutes of clock. Leigh Tiffin, who had missed two earlier field goals,

Above: Running back Mark Ingram (22) stiff-arms a Kentucky defender after picking up 36 yards on a run during the first half. *The Tuscaloosa News | Jason Harless*

Left: Alabama running back Glen Coffee (38) breaks free up the middle for a 78-yard touchdown run during the first quarter as Kentucky defenders pursue. *The Tuscaloosa News | Jason Harless*

Left: Alabama receiver Julio Jones (8) goes up over Kentucky defensive back David Jones to make a reception during the first quarter.
The Tuscaloosa News | Jason Harless
Below: Glen Coffee (38) runs for a touchdown in front of Kentucky's Trevard Lindley in the first quarter.
The Tuscaloosa News | Dan Lopez

hit a 24-yarder to put Alabama ahead 17-7 with 2:04 to play.

The kicked turned out to be the difference in the game.

Kentucky took over and moved to midfield on short passes, then went deep, with quarterback Mike Hartline finding DeMoreo Ford on what Saban called "a blown coverage." The play covered 48 yards, cut the Crimson Tide lead to three points with 40 seconds remaining and set the stage for the onside kick.

Kentucky never had a chance to recover the ball as kicker Lones Seiber's attempt shot harmlessly out of bounds.

The late-game scare overshadowed a huge performance by Coffee, who gained 218 yards — the most by a Southeastern Conference back to this point in the season and the most by a Crimson Tide back since Shaun Alexander's 291-yard effort against LSU in 1996. Coffee did fumble twice in the game, and bobbled a third ball, but provided an early spark and crucial late-game yardage.

"We just decided to batten down the hatches and run the ball," Saban said. "We

Above: Glen Coffee (38) moves the ball upfield for a fourth-quarter first down.
The Tuscaloosa News | Dusty Compton

Top right: Coffee is brought down by a host of Kentucky defenders after a 12-yard gain in the third quarter. *The Tuscaloosa News | Dusty Compton*

Bottom right: Alabama defensive back Justin Woodall (27) attempts to make a tackle on Kentucky running back Derrick Locke during the third quarter
The Tuscaloosa News | Jason Harless

Bottom far right: Alabama receiver Marquis Maze (4) attempts to escape the grasp of Kentucky defender Jeremy Jarmon during the first quarter.
The Tuscaloosa News | Jason Harless

GAME STATS

UA VS. KENTUCKY | OCT. 4, 2008

Score by quarters	1	2	3	4	Final
Kentucky	0	0	7	7	14
Alabama	14	0	0	3	17

Team statistics	Ken.	Ala.
First downs	12	15
— By rush	1	9
— By pass	9	5
— By penalty	2	1
Rushing attempts	35	49
Yds. gained rushing	59	313
Yds. lost rushing	24	31
Net yds. rushing	25	282
Passes attempted	42	17
Passes completed	20	7
Had intercepted	1	4
Net yds. passing	241	106
Total offensive plays	62	66
Total offense	276	388
Avg. gain per play	4.5	5.9
Fumbles-lost	1-1	3-2
Interceptions-yds.	1-0	1-5
Penalties-yds.	9-58	10-92
Punts-yards	10-432	6-259
Yards per punt	43.2	43.2
Punt returns-yds.	2-14	5-52
Kickoff returns-yds.	4-86	1-17
Possession	24:15	35:45
3rd-down conv.	5-17	5-16

AP Top 25

1. Oklahoma (4-0)
2. **Alabama (5-0)**
3. LSU (4-0)
4. Missouri (4-0)
5. Texas (4-0)
6. Penn State (5-0)
7. Texas Tech (4-0)
8. Brigham Young (4-0)
9. USC (2-1)
10. South Florida (5-0)
11. Georgia (4-1)
12. Florida (3-1)
13. Auburn (4-1)
14. Ohio State (4-1)
15. Utah (5-0)
16. Kansas (3-1)
17. Boise State (3-0)
18. Wisconsin (3-1)
19. Vanderbilt (4-0)
20. Virginia Tech (4-1)
21. Oklahoma State (4-0)
22. Fresno State (3-1)
23. Oregon (4-1)
24. Connecticut (5-0)
25. Wake Forest (3-1)

Above : Alabama linebacker Rolando McClain (25) crosses the goal line for a touchdown after recovering a fumble by Kentucky's quarterback during the first quarter. *The Tuscaloosa News | Jason Harless*

Right: Glen Coffee (38) cuts back in an attempt to elude a Kentucky defender during the second quarter. *The Tuscaloosa News | Jason Harless*

weren't doing anything else very well."

That included passing. Quarterback John Parker Wilson hit on just 7 of 17 passes for 106 yards, although two big gainers to Julio Jones were negated by penalties. In that area, Alabama also had its worst game of the year, drawing 10 flags for 92 yards, including several in key situations.

"That's not something we usually do," Wilson said. "We take pride in our execution. It was very uncharacteristic for us."

The Crimson Tide enjoyed statistical dominance of the first half, outgaining the Wildcats by nearly 200 yards. The story of the half, though, came on three plays.

The first came with 10 minutes remaining in the first quarter.

Coffee, reprising his early game-breaking run against Arkansas two weeks before, took the ball to the right side, cleared the first wave of UK defenders and outran the Wildcat secondary for a 78-yard score that put Alabama ahead 7-0.

The second critical play came when Hartline, attempting a screen pass deep in his own territory, dropped the ball for a fumble. Crimson Tide linebacker Rolando McClain scooped it up and went 4 yards for a score with a minute remaining in the first quarter.

Alabama had the Wildcats on the ropes on the ensuing drive, pushing to the Kentucky 6-yard line before Coffee lost a fumble to keep the score at 14-0.

After the half, Saban said, Alabama went "a little flat offensively."

The Crimson Tide had just one first down in the third quarter.

Kentucky had one lightning-quick drive — a pass interference call and two screen passes accounted for 70 yards and a touchdown that cut the UA lead to 14-7 with 5:49 remaining in the quarter.

"We can't have those kinds of letdowns," Saban said. "We need to play with consistency.

"I thought we played hard in a very physical football game. Kentucky is a good team.

"Our team has played very hard over the first six games to get here, and we should give them a lot of credit. But we do have some things we can go back, look at and correct after this game." ■

Above: Alabama linebacker Rolando McClain (25) celebrates with teammates after scoring on a fumble by Kentucky quarterback Mike Hartline during the first quarter.
The Tuscaloosa News | Jason Harless

TIME OUT WITH

#59 ANTOINE CALDWELL

For Alabama center Antoine Caldwell, the low point came the third Saturday in October of his junior year, the day the Crimson Tide played hosted rival Tennessee and he wasn't on the field at Bryant-Denny Stadium.

The night before, Caldwell and four other players had been pulled from the team hotel following an investigation into illicit textbook disbursement. Not only would he not be filling in at right tackle as expected, the players all would sit for four games and helplessly watch the 2007 season fall apart.

"I felt like I had let the team down, big-time," Caldwell said.

It all left a horrible taste in his mouth, compounded by the fact that he was still voted a team captain by those same comrades. With degree in hand, Caldwell could have left the Capstone early for the National Football League, but he couldn't walk away like that, or have that as his legacy.

Caldwell's decision to stay for his senior year turned out to be one of the keys to Alabama's remarkable undefeated regular season in 2008.

"I feel like I had unfinished business," he said. "I just didn't want to have any regret. That's what it was. If I was in the NFL right now, I don't care how much money I was making, if I looked and saw the season Alabama (had), I would be crushed. I hate to say that, but it's true.

"I don't want to live by the 'what if' factor, especially when I knew I could come back here with the team that's going to be good, with a team that definitely had a leader who was taking them to the right place. When I added that all up at the end of the day, the money wouldn't amount to all of that."

Caldwell embraced the leadership role, with fellow lineman Andre Smith

Above: Caldwell snaps the ball against Arkansas State. *The Tuscaloosa News | Robert Sutton*
Left: Caldwell blocks in the first quarter against Georgia. *The Tuscaloosa News | Robert Sutton*
Below left: Caldwell blocks against Arkansas State. *The Tuscaloosa News | Robert Sutton*
Below right: Caldwell snaps the ball in the first quarter against Tulane. *The Tuscaloosa News | Robert Sutton*

nicknaming the Montgomery native 'The Show,' because of the way Caldwell fired up players before every practice.

"It was big (he came back)," Smith said.

Caldwell was named not only first-team All-SEC, but first-team All-American and a finalist for the Rimington Award for the nation's best center, despite being in the same conference as the 2007 winner, Jonathan Luigs of Arkansas.

That wasn't the best part for Caldwell, who also used the extra year to earn a second degree.

"Just seeing how this team has come together, and the younger guys who have come in and contributed, it's been huge," he said. "From the players, to the coaches, to the people around here, everybody. It seems like everyone's having a lot smoother day. Everyone's happier. Everybody's friendlier.

"It's what it's about. It's college football at its finest, and it's why I'm glad I came back." ■

OPPONENT:

OLE MISS

FINAL SCORE: ALABAMA 24 | OLE MISS 20

At halftime of the Alabama-Ole Miss game, Crimson Tide quarterback John Parker Wilson might have envisioned himself watching the final few minutes from the sidelines — but he hardly suspected that his heart would be racing as he pulled for the UA defense to hang on.

The Crimson Tide did hold on for a 24-20 win over Ole Miss, running its record to a perfect 7-0, but only after the Rebels erased almost all of a 21-point halftime deficit. Ole Miss scored 17 unanswered points and took over the football with three minutes remaining, driving into Crimson Tide territory before finally turning the ball over on downs.

Only then did Wilson finally get to take a knee in victory formation, burning off the last 50 seconds.

"We knew if we just got one more score in the second half, we could put them away," Wilson said. "But I don't know what happened. It's been a problem all year. It's not a good feeling, especially when the offense is sitting on the bench at the end and there is nothing you can do about it.

"Fortunately, the defense stopped them and we had made enough plays in the first half."

A week off with an open date the weekend before did nothing to change Alabama's trend of second-half letdowns after a dominant first half, following the pattern of victories over Georgia and Kentucky.

Alabama head coach Nick Saban said that it was "obviously a great win" for the Crimson Tide, but was quick to add that UA was "not just focused on winning."

"It was a big goal to go out and play and (finish) the job in the second half," Saban said. "We didn't do that. Instead, we had a penalty that started their first drive, we didn't do a good job of recognition on a fake field goal, on two occasions we turned the ball over. So we did not exactly get done what we wanted to

Above: Josh Chapman (99) brings down Ole Miss running back Enrique Davis in the second quarter.
The Tuscaloosa News | Dusty Compton

Left: Glen Coffee (38) moves the ball upfield past Ole Miss defenders in the second quarter.
The Tuscaloosa News | Dusty Compton

get done.

"Ole Miss is a really good football team. They do a fantastic job, but we — the coaches and the players — we all need to self-analyze the second half because we aren't getting the job done in these last three games."

Saban's assessment of the Rebels would prove quite accurate as Ole Miss rebounded from the Alabama loss to win its final five games of the regular season to earn a Cotton Bowl bid.

In the end, the Rebels outgained Alabama 359 yards to 326, and only a huge second quarter allowed Alabama to keep its undefeated dream alive.

The first few minutes didn't go exactly according to the normal Alabama script. The Crimson Tide had difficulty establishing its normal running game.

Ole Miss, meanwhile, broke a big play as running back Enrique Davis raced 62 yards to the Crimson Tide 8 midway through the first quarter.

The Alabama defense pushed the Rebels back in the red zone and forced a 25-yard field goal by Joshua Shene. The kick gave Ole Miss a 3-0 lead, the first time all season that Alabama had trailed. That unaccustomed place on the wrong side of the scoreboard, however, lasted just 1 minute and 15 seconds.

Alabama answered with a four-play, 73-yard march, capped by a 26-yard touchdown pass from Wilson to a streaking Marquis Maze with 4:10 left in the quarter.

Alabama found its stride in the second quarter, capitalizing on two Ole Miss turnovers — interceptions by UA safeties Justin Woodall and Rashad Johnson — and scoring 17 points.

Freshman Mark Ingram scored on a 2-yard run to put UA ahead 14-3 with 6:34 left in the half. The interception by Woodall, who grew up just a few miles from the Ole Miss campus, set up a 41-yard Leigh Tiffin

Above: Julio Jones (8) attemts to outrun an Ole Miss defender on a 40-yard reception during the first half. *The Tuscaloosa News | Jason Harless*
Top left: Ole Miss wide receiver Dexter McCluster is swept off his feet by Alabama defenders Brandon Deaderick (95) and Rashad Johnson (49) during the second quarter. *The Tuscaloosa News | Dan Lopez*
Left: Julio Jones (8) applies a stiff-arm to an Ole Miss player.
The Tuscaloosa News | Jason Harless

Above: Ole Miss running back Brandon Bolden is brought down by a host of Alabama defenders on a final drive in the fourth quarter. *The Tuscaloosa News | Dusty Compton*

Above: Alabama receiver Mike McCoy (80) brings in a 30-yard touchdown reception over Ole Miss defender Kendrick Lewis. *The Tuscaloosa News | Jason Harless*

Right: Alabama offensive linemen Marlon Davis (76), Mike Johnson (78) and tight end Nick Walker (88) hold up four fingers at the start of the fourth quarter. *The Tuscaloosa News | Jason Harless*

Right: Running back Glen Coffee (38) is brought down in the third quarter. *The Tuscaloosa News | Dusty Compton*

GAME STATS

UA VS. OLE MISS | OCT. 18, 2008

Score by quarters	1	2	3	4	Final
Ole Miss	3	0	7	10	20
Alabama	7	17	0	0	24

Team statistics	**OM**	**Ala.**
First downs	14	15
— By rush	5	7
— By pass	8	7
— By penalty	1	1
Rushing attempts	34	34
Yds. gained rushing	182	135
Yds. lost rushing	24	28
Net yds. rushing	158	107
Passes attempted	33	25
Passes completed	17	16
Had intercepted	2	2
Net yds. passing	201	219
Total offensive plays	67	59
Total offense	359	326
Avg. gain per play	5.4	5.5
Fumbles-lost	2-1	1-1
Interceptions-yds.	1-11	2-41
Penalties-yds.	4-27	6-55
Punts-yards	5-227	7-278
Yards per punt	45.4	39.7
Punt returns-yds.	5-23	2-14
Kickoff returns-yds.	5-108	5-121
Possession	29:35	29:24
3rd-down conv.	2-14	3-11

AP Top 25

1. Texas (6-0)
2. **Alabama (6-0)**
3. Penn State (7-0)
4. Oklahoma (5-1)
5. Florida (5-1)
6. USC (4-1)
7. Texas Tech (6-0)
8. Oklahoma State (6-0)
9. Brigham Young (6-0)
10. Georgia (5-1)
11. Missouri (5-1)
12. Ohio State (6-1)
13. LSU (4-1)
14. Utah (7-0)
15. Boise State (5-0)
16. Kansas (5-1)
17. Virginia Tech (5-1)
18. North Carolina (5-1)
19. South Florida (5-1)
20. Michigan State (6-1)
21. Wake Forest (4-1)
22. Vanderbilt (5-1)
23. Pittsburgh (4-1)
24. Ball State (7-0)
25. California (4-1)

Above: Alabama's Julio Jones (8) catches a pass for a 40-yard gain in the first quarter.
The Tuscaloosa News | Dusty Compton

Top right: Marquis Maze catches a touchdown pass during the first quarter.
The Tuscaloosa News | Dan Lopez

Right: Alabama tight end Nick Walker (88) moves the ball upfield past an Ole Miss defender in the second quarter for a 40-yard reception.
The Tuscaloosa News | Dusty Compton

field goal to make it 17-3.

Johnson then intercepted a pass attempt off a reverse by Dexter McCluster, returning it 29 yards. Two plays later, Wilson converted a rare UA trick play, taking a lateral from running back Glen Coffee and throwing 30 yards to Mike McCoy on a flea-flicker play for the third Crimson Tide touchdown.

But the big 24-3 halftime lead slowly dwindled. Ole Miss took the second-half kickoff and marched 52 yards for a score, twice converting on fourth down. One of those, the first Rebel touchdown, came on a fake field goal, with holder Rob Park flipping the ball to Jason Cook, who ran for a 9-yard score.

The game stayed at 24-10 until the final 10 minutes. A fumble by Coffee set up the next score, which came on a 17-yard pass from Rebel quarterback Jevan Snead to Shay Hodge.

Alabama went three-and out on its next possession, and the Rebels pulled within four points, 24-20, when Shene knocked a 35-yard field goal off the right upright and through for three points.

Alabama had a chance to burn most of the remaining six minutes, driving for a couple of first downs before stalling. A dropped pass denied the Crimson Tide a possible conversion, and the Rebels took over at their 24 with a chance at a final, potentially game winning, drive.

Ole Miss managed two first downs, thanks mainly to Snead's scrambling, and drove to the Alabama 43. But on fourth-and-five, Snead's pass to McCluster fell harmlessly short.

"Our guys came back in the second half after not having a very good first half," said Ole Miss coach Houston Nutt. "We hurt ourselves with a penalty at a bad time and a fumble at a bad time. You just can't do that and beat a No. 2 team in the country."

Alabama noseguard Terrence Cody was injured in the third quarter and was taken from the field. Saban indicated that the junior had suffered a ligament injury and would be out "one or two weeks," but added that an MRI would be necessary to confirm the diagnosis. ■

VOLS
VOLS
SEC

OPPONENT:

TENNESSEE

FINAL SCORE: ALABAMA 29 | TENNESSEE 9

It is a series that has produced its share of magical moments — but this wasn't magical, just methodical.

The University of Alabama Crimson Tide pounded its ancient rival without mercy at Neyland Stadium, stifling the Tennessee Volunteers 29-9 and running the season record to 8-0.

This time there was no second-half letdown, only a four-quarter beat-down.

It was the Crimson Tide's second straight victory over Tennessee, the first winning streak for UA against the Vols since the 1992 victory capped a run of seven straight wins. It was also the first time since 1974 and '75 that Alabama had whipped Tennessee by 20 points or more in consecutive meetings.

The game also set the stage for the dismissal of Tennessee's longtime head coach, Phillip Fulmer, before the season's end. Fulmer joined Clemson's Terry Bowden on the list of coaches who lost to Alabama and won't be back at their respective schools next season, a list that would continue to grow.

"This is the best we've played, in my opinion, since the Clemson game," Crimson Tide head coach Nick Saban said. "In the Georgia game we played a good half, but tonight was a complete effort and it needed to be.

"I've never been prouder of our team, our players and the way they competed."

The Alabama defense held UT to just 173 total yards — only 36 on the ground — and 10 first downs.

"I don't know what happened to our running game," Fulmer

Above: Defensive back Kareem Jackson (3) brings down a Tennessee wide receiver after a catch in the second quarter. *The Tuscaloosa News | Dusty Compton*
Left: Glen Coffee (38) dives over the goal line for a touchdown in the second quarter. *The Tuscaloosa News | Dusty Compton*

Above: Rolando McClain (25) brings down a Tennessee wide receiver in the third quarter. *The Tuscaloosa News | Dusty Compton*
Top right: The Crimson Tide takes the field. *The Tuscaloosa News | Dusty Compton*
Far right: Tennessee fans hide in defeat. *The Tuscaloosa News | Jason Harless*
Right: Julio Jones (8) gives a stiff-arm to a Tennessee defender in the third quarter. *The Tuscaloosa News | Jason Harless*

said. "It's as disappointing as can be."

The Crimson Tide had two serious errors in the kicking game in the first half, but survived relatively unscathed.

Alabama took the early lead, taking the opening kickoff and driving to the UT 22, where Leigh Tiffin converted on a 39-yard field goal.

Alabama held the Vols on the ensuing possession, but the first special-teams miscue led to UT points. Returner Javier Arenas fumbled the Volunteers' punt at the Alabama 5-yard line, where UT recovered.

The Crimson Tide defense pushed Tennessee back to the 12-yard line, but Jeremy Lincoln kicked a 31-yard field goal, tying the score at 3-3 with 6:29 remaining in the first quarter.

Tennessee reciprocated, approximately, later in the quarter when Britton Colquitt shanked a punt to give the Crimson Tide possession at the Volunteer 47.

A 14-yard completion from John Parker Wilson to Julio Jones put UA in field-goal range and Tiffin converted from 43 yards out.

Alabama pushed its lead to 13-3 late in the second quarter, taking over after a missed UT field goal and driving 66 yards.

Glen Coffee went over on a fourth-and-one from the 3-yard line, pushing the Crimson Tide lead to 10 points, 13-3, with 2:41 to go in the half.

Above: Alabama's John Parker Wilson (14) and Baron Huber (40) celebrate after a third-quarter touchdown.
The Tuscaloosa News | Robert Sutton

Left: Rashad Johnson (49) breaks up a pass intended for Tennessee receiver Denarius Moore (6) in the third quarter.
The Tuscaloosa News | Dusty Compton

Left: Glen Coffee (38) dives across the goal line for an Alabama touchdown as a Tennessee defender attempts to make a tackle during the second quarter.

The Tuscaloosa News | Jason Harless

INSIDE THE GAME

It didn't seem right that the person who initiated the longest offensive play for the Alabama Crimson Tide in Neyland Stadium didn't get to enjoy it.

Quarterback John Parker Wilson didn't mind, especially considering that true freshman wide receiver Julio Jones made the impressive sideline catch on a fade route for a 35-yard gain.

"I didn't even see it. I was on the ground," Wilson said. "It was a big part of the game. We knew we had to come out and score."

Four plays later, the Crimson Tide did exactly that on a 3-yard touchdown run by junior running back Glen Coffee, and Alabama never looked back.

"We really prepared hard and were focused," junior left tackle Andre Smith said. "It showed today."

Alabama had huge advantages in every statistical category. The Tide scored all four times it had the ball inside the UT 20, ran almost 20 more plays than the Volunteers and blew away Tennessee on the ground, 178 yards to just 36.

The key was that Alabama had to get Tennessee on its heels, and do so against one of the top defenses in the nation. The Tide took a page from last year's 41-17 victory over the Vols at Bryant-Denny Stadium, using the pass to set up the run — especially during the first touchdown drive.

With Alabama up 6-3 with 5:44 remaining in the half, Jones started it with a 19-yard gain on a crossing route, followed by the fade down to the Tennessee 12. He went on finish with six receptions for 103 yards, his best collegiate outing to that point.

"They had a very good defensive team, and I was very pleased with the way the offense was able to move the football," Alabama head coach Nick Saban said. "We had good balance. John Parker played an outstanding game."

Through the first three games away from Bryant-Denny Stadium, Wilson had completed 41 of 60 passes for 459 yards, four touchdowns and no interceptions. His completion percentage was 68.3 percent.

He proved to be true to form against Tennessee, completing 17 of 24 passes for 188 yards (70.8 percent).

Wilson didn't have any passing touchdowns, but more important were the zero turnovers by the offense.

"The way the defense was playing, we just kept the ball, didn't turn it over," Wilson said. "It's great to leave Knoxville with a win." ■

Left: A Tennessee runner is brought down by Alabama's Lorenzo Washington (97) in the first quarter. *The Tuscaloosa News | Dusty Compton*

Below: Nick Saban gives a thumbs-up to fans after Alabama's 29-9 victory. *The Tuscaloosa News | Jason Harless*

Far left: Fan Taylor Fortinberry celebrates Alabama's victory over Tennessee with a cigar. *The Tuscaloosa News | Jason Harless*

Left: Roy Upchurch (5) goes down just short of the end zone in the third quarter. *The Tuscaloosa News | Robert Sutton*

GAME STATS

UA VS. TENNESSEE | OCT. 25, 2008

Score by quarters	1	2	3	4	Final
Alabama	6	7	9	7	29
Tennessee	3	0	0	6	9

Team statistics	**Ala.**	**UT**
First downs	23	20
— By rush	11	4
— By pass	10	4
— By penalty	2	2
Rushing attempts	43	21
Yds. gained rushing	187	57
Yds. lost rushing	9	21
Net yds. rushing	178	36
Passes attempted	24	28
Passes completed	17	16
Had intercepted	0	0
Net yds. passing	188	137
Total offensive plays	67	49
Total offense	366	173
Avg. gain per play	5.5	3.5
Fumbles-lost	1-1	0-0
Interceptions-yds.	0-0	0-0
Penalties-yds.	3-35	7-60
Punts-yards	3-144	7-306
Yards per punt	38.0	43.7
Punt returns-yds.	3-17	1-(-1)
Kickoff returns-yds.	3-50	7-134
Possession	35:32	24:28
3rd-down conv.	4-13	3-13

AP Top 25

1. Texas (7-0)
2. **Alabama (7-0)**
3. Penn State (8-0)
4. Oklahoma (6-1)
5. Florida (5-1)
6. USC (5-1)
7. Oklahoma State (7-0)
8. Texas Tech (7-0)
9. Georgia (6-1)
10. Ohio State (7-1)
11. LSU (5-1)
12. Utah (8-0)
13. Boise State (6-0)
14. South Florida (6-1)
15. TCU (7-1)
16. Missouri (5-2)
17. Pittsburgh (5-1)
18. Brigham Young (6-1)
19. Kansas (5-2)
20. Ball State (7-0)
21. Georgia Tech (6-1)
22. Tulsa (7-0)
23. Boston College (5-1)
24. Florida State (5-1)
25. Minnesota (6-1)

BCS Top 10

1. Texas
2. **Alabama**
3. Penn State
4. Oklahoma
5. USC
6. Oklahoma State
7. Georgia
8. Texas Tech
9. Ohio State
10. Florida

Left: Members of the Alabama defense gang-tackle a Tennessee running back on a third-and-short during the first quarter.
The Tuscaloosa News | Jason Harless

Tennessee drove deep into Alabama territory as the half expired, but Lincoln missed a 43-yard field goal on the final play of the half.

"The defense did a great job twice in the game," Saban said. "Both kicking-game errors — the fumble that gave them the ball inside the 5-yard line and getting out of there with a field goal; and the partially blocked punt down there and getting out of there with no points — right there, that was a great job of getting out of there with no points allowed.

"On the fourth-and-[illegible] ball, my thing it's inside the 5 and it's one (yard) or less, I believe in our guys, and they came through."

Unlike the previous three weeks, Alabama continued the domination into the second half, pulling away from the Volunteers.

Tiffin added his third field goal, a 30-yarder, on the first Crimson Tide possession of the second half.

Wilson, who had one of his most efficient games, completing 17 of 24 passes for 186 yards, added a 1-yard touchdown run later in the quarter.

Roy Upchurch, who rushed for 86 yards, all in the second half, capped the Crimson Tide scoring with a 4-yard scoring run early in the fourth quarter.

Tennessee added a late touchdown, a small consolation for the remnants of the crowd of 106,138. Josh Briscoe scored on a 10-yard pass from Nick Stephens with 7:26 remaining, but Alabama was able to control the ball for the rest of the game.

Crimson Tide freshman wide receiver Jones had his first career 100-yard receiving game, catching six passes for 103 yards. It was the first 100-yard receiving game for Alabama since last season, when DJ Hall turned the trick against Tennessee in Tuscaloosa. ■

WALKER

OPPONENT:

ARKANSAS STATE

FINAL SCORE: ALABAMA 35 | ARKANSAS STATE 0

The University of Alabama adopted the simplest formula to snap its long losing streak in November football games. Just don't let the other team score.

The Crimson Tide blanked Arkansas State 35-0 to record its first month-of-November win in three years. Ironically, the shutout for the UA defense was the first since that win, a 17-0 victory over Mississippi State in Starkville on Nov. 5, 2005.

Freshman Mark Ingram ran for 113 yards on 12 carries and scored two touchdowns in the game. Quarterback John Parker Wilson completed 15 of 28 passes for 152 yards, throwing one interception.

But it was the defense, which limited ASU to 158 total yards, that carried the day.

"It's huge when the defense plays like that," Wilson said. "They shut out the other team, they score a touchdown. When the defense is playing like that, our job is just not to turn the ball over and play smart."

Alabama dominated from the outset, but a couple of instances of red-zone inefficiency on offense in the first half kept the score relatively close.

The Crimson Tide took its first possession and marched 89 yards for a touchdown, with Glen Coffee capping the drive with a 9-yard touchdown run.

Those were the only offensive points of the half, however.

"We moved the ball on down in the red zone and threw an interception," UA head coach Nick Saban said. "Then it's the same as a turnover when we sputter in the two-minute offense and miss a field goal.

"I get really frustrated when we don't score in those situations. I also get frustrated when we let them score. So I stay frustrated a lot.

"Today, I was pleased with the way the guys kind of ground it out."

The Crimson Tide did add another first-half score, but it came courtesy of the defense as safety Rashad Johnson intercepted a Corey Leonard pass and returned it 32 yards for a touchdown. It was the fourth defensive touchdown of the season for

Left: Glen Coffee looks for an opening in the first quarter.
The Tuscaloosa News | Michael E. Palmer

Opposite page: Roy Upchurch (5) runs for a touchdown in the third quarter.
The Tuscaloosa News | Dan Lopez

Above: Glen Coffee (38) crosses the goal line ahead of an Arkansas State defender on a 9-yard touchdown run during the first quarter.
The Tuscaloosa News | Jason Harless
Top right: Mark Ingram attempts to break the tackle of Arkansas State defenders during the third quarter.
The Tuscaloosa News | Jason Harless
Right: Alabama's John Parker Wilson (14) prepares to throw a pass.
The Tuscaloosa News | Robert Sutton
Far right: Wilson is sacked by Arkansas State during the third quarter.
The Tuscaloosa News | Jason Harless
Opposite page: Glen Coffee (38) scores a first-quarter touchdown.
The Tuscaloosa News | Robert Sutton

GAME STATS

UA VS. ARK. STATE | NOV. 1, 2008

Score by quarters	1	2	3	4	Final
Ark. State	0	0	0	0	0
Alabama	7	7	14	7	35

Team statistics	ASU	Ala.
First downs	11	21
— By rush	6	12
— By pass	3	8
— By penalty	2	1
Rushing attempts	37	36
Yds. gained rushing	138	228
Yds. lost rushing	47	23
Net yds. rushing	91	205
Passes attempted	17	28
Passes completed	8	15
Had intercepted	1	1
Net yds. passing	67	152
Total offensive plays	54	64
Total offense	158	357
Avg. gain per play	2.9	5.6
Fumbles-lost	1-0	1-0
Interceptions-yds.	1-23	1-32
Penalties-yds.	7-73	3-33
Punts-yards	7-259	3-121
Yards per punt	37.0	40.3
Punt returns-yds.	2-5	4-27
Kickoff returns-yds.	5-96	1-13
Possession	31:59	28:01
3rd-down conv.	2-12	8-13

AP Top 25
1. Texas (8-0)
2. **Alabama (8-0)**
3. Penn State (9-0)
4. Oklahoma (7-1)
5. Florida (6-1)
6. Texas Tech (8-0)
7. USC (6-1)
8. Georgia (7-1)
9. Oklahoma State (7-1)
10. Utah (8-0)
11. Boise State (7-0)
12. TCU (8-1)
13. Ohio State (7-2)
14. Missouri (6-2)
15. LSU (5-2)
16. Florida State (6-1)
17. Brigham Young (7-1)
18. Ball State (8-0)
19. Tulsa (8-0)
20. Minnesota (7-1)
21. North Carolina (6-2)
22. Michigan State (7-2)
23. Oregon (6-2)
24. South Florida (6-2)
25. Maryland (6-2)

BCS Top 10
1. Texas
2. **Alabama**
3. Penn State
4. Oklahoma
5. USC
6. Georgia
7. Texas Tech
8. Florida
9. Oklahoma State
10. Utah

Left: Alabama reciever Mike McCoy runs with the ball against Arkansas State. *The Tuscaloosa News | Robert Sutton*
Below: Alabama defensive back Rashad Johnson (49) crosses the goal line after returning an interception for a touchdown during the second quarter. *The Tuscaloosa News | Jason Harless*
Left center: Coach Nick Saban looks over the game action from the sidelines. *The Tuscaloosa News | Robert Sutton*
Left bottom: Rashad Johnson eludes a diving tackle attempt by an Arkansas State receiver during the second quarter. *The Tuscaloosa News | Jason Harless*

Left: Roy Upchurch (5) celebrates a touchdown with Baron Huber (40).
The Tuscaloosa News | Robert Sutton

Below: Receiver Julio Jones (8) cuts upfield after making a reception during the second quarter.
The Tuscaloosa News | Jason Harless

Alabama.

The UA defense limited the Red Wolves to just 56 yards in the first half.

In the second half, Alabama improved its offensive productivity, scoring two third-quarter touchdowns.

Alabama took the kickoff after halftime and marched 70 yards for a score. Roy Upchurch capped the march with a 22-yard touchdown run. Later in the quarter, Ingram became the third Crimson Tide tailback to score in the game, driving in from the 5-yard line.

Ingram capped the scoring with 4:37 to play, picking up his second touchdown on a 17-yard run.

"It's great for the defense any time you shut a team out," Saban said. "It says a lot about the job that Kirby (Smart) and Kevin (Steele) have done, along with the entire defensive staff because (Arkansas State) was a pretty good offensive football team."

Still, Saban said he saw "room for improvement" in Alabama's performance.

"First, we didn't pass the ball as well as we would like," Saban said. "They played a little matchup coverage that forced John Parker to hold the ball longer than he would like, and then there were times that they played man-to-man when our receivers didn't get open. It is something we will keep working on."

Wilson concurred with Saban's assessment of the passing game.

"We were just a little off, nothing big, just a little bit here and a little bit there," he said.

Alabama improved to 9-0 and extended its winning streak to 10 straight games -- dating back to the Independence Bowl victory over Colorado at the end of the 2007 season — for the first time since the 1994 season. ■

TIME OUT WITH #49 RASHAD JOHNSON

Rashad Johnson arrived at the University of Alabama as a seventh-string running back without a scholarship. He left with All-America honors at safety.

The 6-foot, 186-pound player from Sulligent had scholarship offers from Division II schools out of high school, and even an offer to play junior college basketball, but he elected to walk on at Alabama and earn his way.

Even through the tough times, Johnson never regretted that decision.

"The best ting about the path is that it wasn't easy," Johnson said. "I think it makes you more humble and more loving of what you're doing when you don't have it as easy as some of the other guys did to get to where you're at.

"Having to come in and walk on and work for everything to get a scholarship, it's just been a constant fight. It just makes me love what I do even more."

In the 2008 season, Johnson finished second on the team in tackles and made five interceptions, including three against LSU in a game that earned him national defensive player of the week honors.

He was on the watch list for the Bronko Nagurski Trophy and the Jim Thorpe Award, two of college football's top defensive honors, and was even named Defensive Player of the Year in the Southeastern Conference by the Little Rock (Ark.) Touchdown Club.

It wasn't Johnson's highlights that made him special, however. It

Above: Rashad Johnson (49) breaks up a pass in the Tennessee game.
The Tuscaloosa News | Dusty Compton
Top left: Johnson jumps high in an interception attempt agains Clemson.
The Tuscaloosa News | Dusty Compton
Left: Johnson (49) carries the ball against Arkansas State.
The Tuscaloosa News | Dan Lopez
Far left: Johnson makes a tackle on on a Kentucky running back.
The Tuscaloosa News | Jason Harless
Opposite page: Johnson returns an interception for a touchdown against LSU. *The Tuscaloosa News | Michael E. Palmer*

was his heady play and knowledge of the game.

"They've got a safety who makes the right read on every play and gets into position to make every play the way you're supposed to make it," Florida coach Urban Meyer said.

That Johnson made it to Alabama at all was a long shot.

He chose a Bible verse for his yearbook entry at Sulligent High School, II Timothy 1:7, which he later had tattooed on his arm: "For God hath not given us the spirit of fear; but of power, and of love, and of a sound mind."

Johnson chose the path of no fear, but needed help. One of his junior high coaches, Thomas Howell, was a former walk-on at Alabama. He contacted the UA coaching staff and helped Johnson get enrolled as a non-scholarship football player. The player's parents put off buying a new car and cut other expenses to pay his tuition.

The turning point came when former Alabama head coach Mike Shula asked Johnson to move to safety and awarded him a scholarship before his sophomore year.

Johnson graduated in the summer before his senior season. Of 15 non-scholarship players who joined the program at the same time he did, Johnson was the last one still around by his senior season.

The player doesn't dwell on his success, but sometimes marvels at how things turned out.

"It's just crazy to be able to do what I've done," he said. "It's a blessing. This is just a crazy outcome to what I set out to accomplish." ■

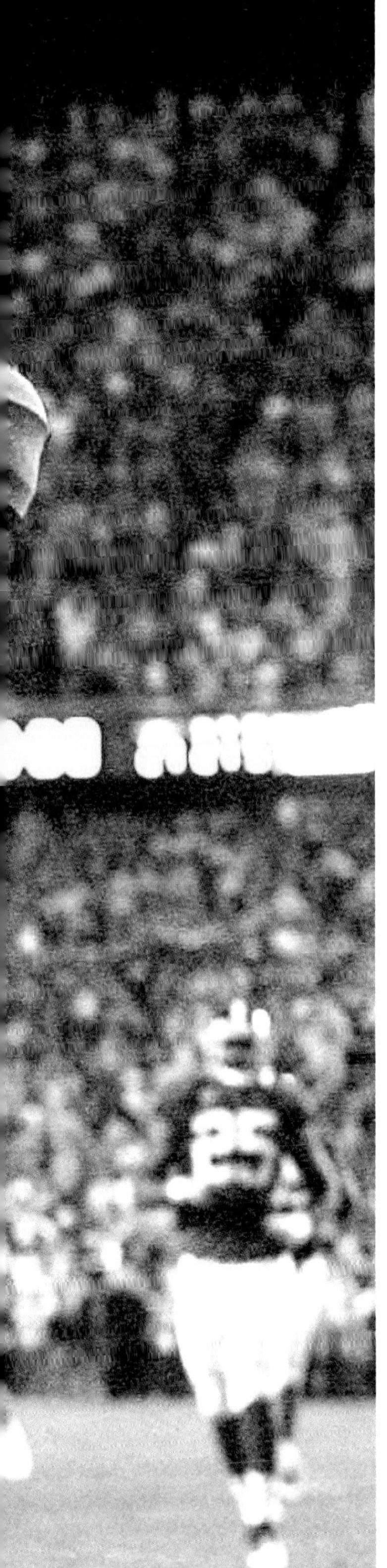

OPPONENT:

LOUISIANA STATE UNIVERSITY

FINAL SCORE: ALABAMA 27 | LSU 21

It was like he never left.

Nick Saban came back to Tiger Stadium and did the same thing with his current team, the Alabama Crimson Tide, as he used to do when he stood on the other sideline when he was head coach of the LSU Tigers.

Saban's No. 1-ranked Alabama team took a 27-21 overtime victory over LSU, assuring a trip to the Southeastern Conference Championship Game and disappointing a record crowd of 93,039, most of whom were lusting for Saban's blood for most of the game.

Instead, the Tigers were left with the bitter taste of ashes, done in by Alabama's tenacity, the sure hands of Rashad Johnson and Julio Jones and, to be fair, the Tigers' own mistakes as well.

"Our players overcame a lot of adversity," said Crimson Tide head coach Nick Saban, who has now won 12 straight games at Tiger Stadium, dating back to his LSU tenure.

It took an overtime to overcome the last little bit, but the Crimson Tide made the big plays in the extra period.

LSU had the first possession, but it ended when senior safety Johnson intercepted Jarrett Lee, the Tigers' freshman quarterback, in the end zone.

"It's a throw that he does not need to make," Les Miles, the LSU coach, said. "But his view was, 'I hit this one, we win.' Boy, what a great view. I just need to coach him some more, love him,

Above: From left, Brian Motley (66), Glen Coffee (38) and Mike Johnson (78) walk off the field after beating LSU. *The Tuscaloosa News | Dan Lopez*

Left: Alabama's Rashad Johnson (49), right, makes his third interception in the game against LSU during overtime. *The Tuscaloosa News | Dan Lopez*

support him and make him better."

After the interception, Alabama chose to go for the swift knockout..

"As I was going on the field, Coach Saban said, 'Let's take a shot,'" quarterback John Parker Wilson said. "Of course, we threw it to Julio (Jones)."

The Crimson Tide's freshman receiver, who had seven catches for 128 yards, hauled the ball in at the 1. The Crimson Tide then took two cracks at the end zone, with Wilson sneaking in for the game-winner on second down.

"When we're that close, we want to punch it in," Wilson said. "We just want to take all the chance out of it,"

The touchdown gave Alabama its first win over LSU since the 2002 season, when Saban was coaching at LSU.

Saban's return was greeted with loud boos, but the Crimson Tide coach also mentioned that many LSU fans had welcomed his return.

"I really appreciate that," Saban said. "We have special memories of this place, and no one will tarnish those, no matter what they do."

Alabama came back to win despite what Saban called "the most lethargic (first) half we have played all year."

The first half was filled with errors on both sides, starting with Alabama's opening series.

The Crimson Tide sliced through the LSU defense after taking the opening kickoff, but the drive ended when Earl Alexander, after catching a pass from a scrambling Wilson, fumbled as he stretched for the goal line.

The ball rolled out of the end zone for a touchback, giving LSU possession and wasting an Alabama scoring threat.

The Crimson Tide committed two more turnovers, including a fumbled punt return by Javier Arenas that set up the second LSU touchdown, a 30-yard run by Charles Scott.

But Lee, the interception-plagued Tiger rookie, was picked off for the equalizer, a

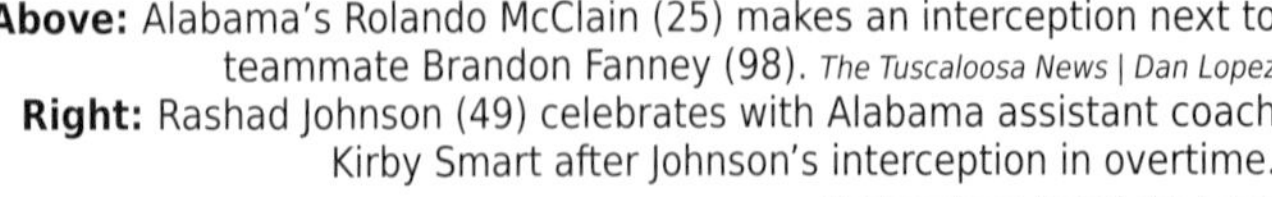

Above: Alabama's Rolando McClain (25) makes an interception next to teammate Brandon Fanney (98). *The Tuscaloosa News | Dan Lopez*

Right: Rashad Johnson (49) celebrates with Alabama assistant coach Kirby Smart after Johnson's interception in overtime. *The Tuscaloosa News | Dan Lopez*

Top right: LSU football fans watch as an effigy of Alabama football head coach Nick Saban burns during a rally in Baton Rouge prior to the game. *The Tuscaloosa News | Dan Lopez*

Above: Alabama's Julio Jones (8) attempts to shake off LSU defenders after a reception in the first quarter.
The Tuscaloosa News | Michael E. Palmer
Far left: A painted LSU fan looks on as Alabama beats the Tigers.
The Tuscaloosa News | Michael E. Palmer
Left: Dejected LSU fans watch the Crimson Tide win.
The Tuscaloosa News | Dan Lopez

INSIDE THE GAME

The ending was as anticlimactic as the game was dramatic as the top-ranked Alabama Crimson Tide defeated No. 15 LSU in overtime at Tiger Stadium.

For all the drama that went before it, the overtime finish was settled by two monumental plays that gave Alabama a major victory to highlight its perfect record.

Alabama seemed deflated, if not downright defeated, going into the extra period after two near misses in the final three minutes that left the game tied at the end of regulation.

John Parker Wilson's 32-yard touchdown scramble was called back by a holding penalty and Leigh Tiffin's 29-yard field goal try on the last play of regulation was blocked, leaving Alabama reeling on the brink of collapse.

Instead, the Tide shook it off and took command of the overtime.

"You've got to keep playing and play the next play no matter what happened on the last play," Tide coach Nick Saban said. "That's what we asked the players to do."

Alabama won the overtime coin toss and elected to play defense first. LSU netted four yards on two running plays, putting the Tigers in a passing situation on third-and-six. The Tide was ready.

"We told the defensive players when they went out there for overtime, you've got to make a play, you've got to get them stopped and we'll win the game," Saban said.

Senior safety Rashad Johnson made that play, intercepting LSU quarterback Jarrett Lee in the end zone to snuff out LSU's overtime possession.

Lee had been successful three times in the second half on plays where he rolled to the right and passed to a target running downfield in front of him.

Alabama anticipated the Tigers going back to the play and blitzed to force a quick throw. Johnson shadowed the receiver and picked off the pass.

"I was just trying to do everything I could to help my team out," Johnson said. "I saw him roll out, and it was just a great play call for us to blitz him on that side so he couldn't get all the way out and throw the out route like he normally does.

"He looked for the seven (points) and he overthrew him."

Stopping LSU was only half the job. Alabama still had to score to win the game.

Wilson silenced LSU's raucous fans on the Tide's first overtime snap. Operating from the shotgun, he purposefully threw a pass a little behind freshman wideout Julio Jones, who was running down the left sideline. Jones shook the coverage of LSU's Patrick Peterson to come back to the ball for the catch, then turned upfield toward the goal line. Peterson held on to drag him down a yard short of the end zone for a 24-yard gain.

"We decided to go with a big play right off the bat and went to Julio," Saban said, "which we hit one play down there, and that makes a big difference."

Wilson said the play was going to Jones, "all the way."

Said Wilson, "He made a great play. It was a back-shoulder ball, great adjustment. He was able to beat them out."

Two plays later Wilson sneaked the ball across the goal line for the game-winning score.

"We struggled to get it in, but we got it in," Saban said. ■

Above: Nick Saban jogs out of Tiger Stadium in Baton Rouge after No.1-ranked Alabama defeated LSU 27-21 in overtime. *The Tuscaloosa News | Michael E. Palmer*

Above: LSU players react at the goal line after Alabama quarterback John Parker Wilson's game-winning touchdown. *The Tuscaloosa News | Michael E. Palmer*

Above: Alabama's Julio Jones (8) makes one of his seven catches for 128 yards.
The Tuscaloosa News | Michael E. Palmer

GAME STATS

UA VS. LSU | NOV. 8, 2008

Score by quarters	1	2	3	4	OT	F
Alabama	7	7	7	0	6	27
LSU	14	0	0	7	0	21

Team statistics	Ala.	LSU
First downs	16	17
— By rush	7	8
— By pass	8	9
— By penalty	1	0
Rushing attempts	37	46
Yds. gained rushing	147	213
Yds. lost rushing	9	12
Net yds. rushing	138	201
Passes attempted	31	34
Passes completed	15	13
Had intercepted	1	4
Net yds. passing	215	181
Total offensive plays	68	80
Total offense	353	382
Avg. gain per play	5.2	4.8
Fumbles-lost	3-2	0-0
Interceptions-yds.	4-76	1-0
Penalties-yds.	2-24	5-32
Punts-yards	7-295	8-321
Yards per punt	42.1	40.1
Punt returns-yds.	3-23	2-25
Kickoff returns-yds.	4-79	4-86
Possession	26:40	33:20
3rd-down conv.	4-13	5-19

AP Top 25

1. **Alabama (9-0)**
2. Texas Tech (9-0)
3. Penn State (9-0)
4. Florida (7-1)
5. Texas (8-1)
6. Oklahoma (8-1)
7. USC (7-1)
8. Oklahoma State (8-1)
9. Boise State (8-0)
10. Utah (9-0)
11. TCI (9-1)
12. Ohio State (7-2)
13. Missouri (7-2)
14. Georgia (7-2)
15. LSU (6-2)
16. Ball State (8-0)
17. Brigham Young (8-1)
18. Michigan State (8-2)
19. North Carolina (6-2)
20. West Virginia (6-2)
21. California (6-2)
22. Georgia Tech (7-2)
23. Maryland (6-2)
24. Florida State (6-2)
25. Pittsburgh (6-2)

BCS Top 10

1. **Alabama**
2. Texas Tech
3. Penn State
4. Texas
5. Florida
6. Oklahoma
7. USC
8. Utah
9. Oklahoma State
10. Boise State

56-yard Johnson return for a touchdown that knotted the game at 14-14.

Johnson finished with three interceptions in the nationally-televised game and won national defensive player of the week honors.

LSU had a chance to take the lead in the final seconds of the first half, but Colt David missed a 41-yard field-goal attempt.

It was the first time in the season that Alabama did not lead by at least 10 points at the end of the first half.

The Crimson Tide scored a go-ahead touchdown with 8:14 remaining in the third quarter.

Glen Coffee set up the score with a 23-yard run down to the 3-yard line, then took the ball from there for the touchdown.

Coffee finished the game with 126 yards on 26 carries.

LSU answered in the fourth quarter as Scott scored his second touchdown, a 1-yard run, with 6:12 to play.

The two teams exchanged possessions, but a strong punt return by Arenas set Alabama up in LSU territory.

The Crimson Tide drove as far as the LSU 11-yard line, but Leigh Tiffin's 29-yard field goal attempt to win the game was blocked by the Tigers' Ricky Jean Francois as time expired.

That set the stage for Alabama's overtime win.

It also kept the 10-0 Crimson Tide's national championship hopes alive, proving to detractors that Alabama could overcome adversity, although Saban said it was premature to discuss such matters.

"We are at about 19,000 feet," Saban said, "The mountain is at 26,000 feet. The air is getting a little rarer and you have to change how you breathe sometimes, but you still have to focus on the task at hand. If you slip up, the consequences can be devastating, even more so than when you are at 7,000 feet." ■

Above: Glen Coffee (38) makes a run with the ball during the third quarter. *The Tuscaloosa News | Dan Lopez*

Right: Julio Jones (8) moves the ball toward the end zone after a 24-yard reception in overtime. *The Tuscaloosa News | Michael E. Palmer*

22
52
STATE

OPPONENT:

MISSISSIPPI STATE UNIVERSITY

FINAL SCORE: ALABAMA 32 | MSU 7

It was only appropriate for a University of Alabama football team in the final stages of fashioning a special season to have its special teams to thank for this win.

Big plays in the kicking game sustained Alabama in the early going against Mississippi State before the Crimson Tide finally wore down the Bulldogs and pulled away for a 32-7 win.

The victory snapped a two-year losing streak against Sylvester Croom and the Bulldogs and extended the No. 1-ranked Crimson Tide's winning streak to 12 games, 11 in this unbeaten season.

Croom, a Tuscaloosa native and former Alabama All-American, resigned his position two weeks later after a one-sided loss to Ole Miss.

Alabama blocked a punt for a safety and got a record-setting performance from punt returner Javier Arenas.

Arenas set up the first Crimson Tide touchdown with a 46-yard punt return, then put the game away with an 80-yard touchdown return in the third quarter.

With 153 yards on six returns, Arenas shattered his own school record for single-game punt return yardage, set earlier in the season against Tulane.

Placekicker Leigh Tiffin, bouncing back from a sub-par performance against LSU a week earlier, was perfect on three field-goal attempts.

"Special teams, as much as any game this year, had a huge impact on field position," said Crimson Tide head coach Nick Saban. "Javier Arenas and the return teams had a tremendous impact on this game. The specialists did a tremendous job of controlling vertical field position.

Right: Alabama receiver Julio Jones attempts to elude Mississippi State defenders after making a reception during the first quarter. *The Tuscaloosa News | Jason Harless*

Left: Alabama running back Mark Ingram hurdles teammate Mike Johnson as defenders close in during the fourth quarter. *The Tuscaloosa News | Jason Harless*

"Special teams was a real key in the game today."

Alabama led by just five points at halftime, but outscored MSU 20-0 in the second half.

"The first half, we didn't play especially well," Saban said. "We made a lot of mental errors, which is not like us. We had a lot of energy, but we didn't play smart.

"Javy's second return (for the 80-yard touchdown) probably changed momentum as much as anything."

Alabama headed into an extra week to prepare for rival Auburn off the Mississippi State win.

"We've got a lot of guys that are nicked up, beat up and bruised up. No one ever knows if a bye week is a good time or bad time, but I look at our team and think this is a good time for us to get a lot of rest.

"We're tired emotionally. They play with a lot of intangibles and challenge themselves," Saban said.

Alabama started the scoring after a precise punt by P.J. Fitzgerald pinned Mississippi State at its 1-yard line on its first possession. The Bulldogs were unable to move, and Blake McAdams' punt attempt from his own end zone was blocked by the Crimson Tide's Kareem Jackson for a safety and a 2-0 lead with 10:03 remaining in the first quarter.

"We went after the kick," Saban said. "They actually lost their snapper somewhere along the way and we saw that, so we said we would go after it and the snap was a little high. Kareem came off the corner and got it."

The Crimson Tide pushed the lead to 5-0 on a 35-yard field goal by Tiffin with 1:43 remaining in the quarter.

Mississippi State actually took the lead briefly in the second quarter, putting together its best two offensive plays — a 32-yard pass from Tyson Lee to Arnil Stallworth and a 31-yard touchdown pass from Lee

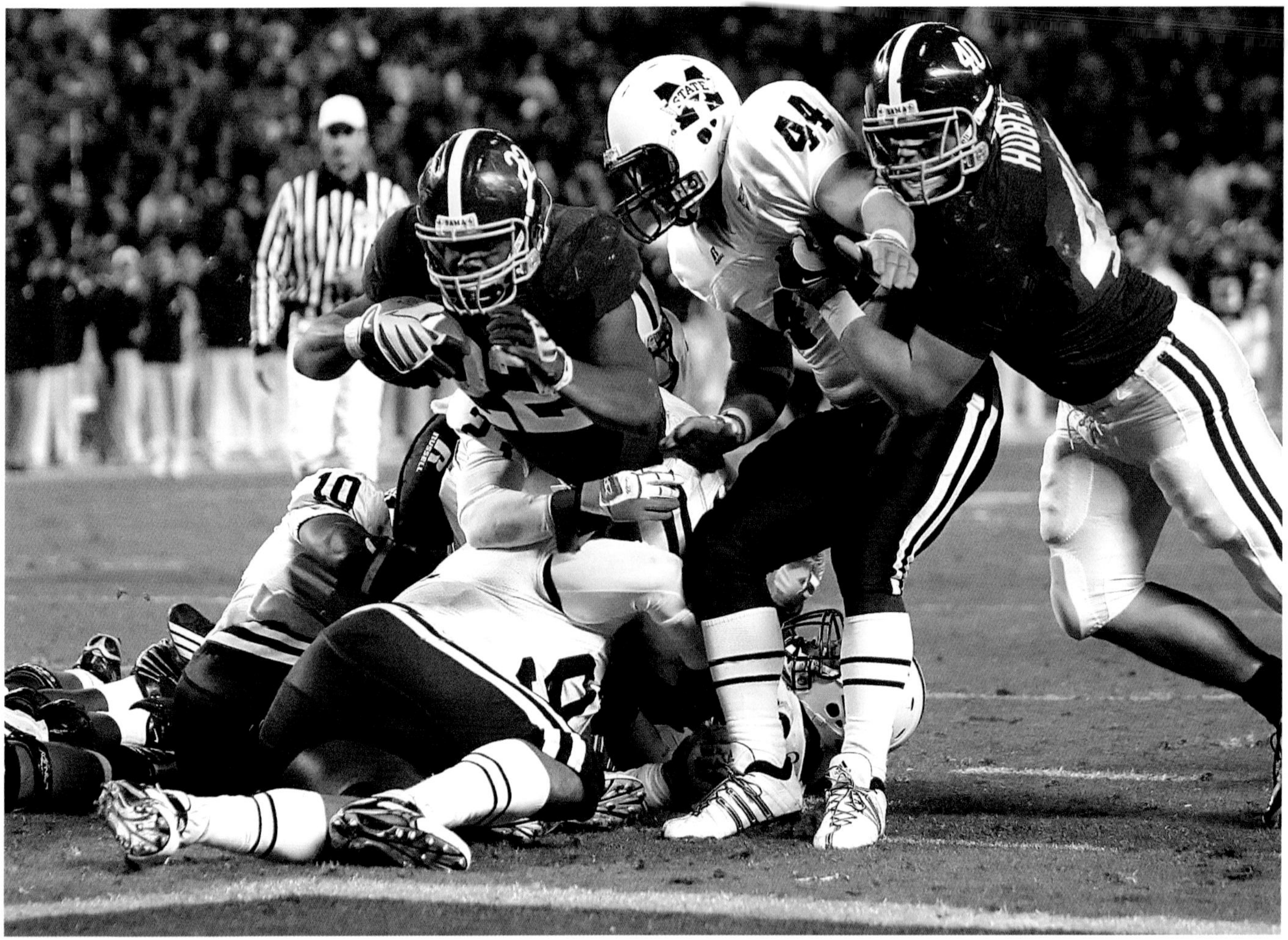

Above: Alabama running back Mark Ingram (22) dives over the line of scrimmage for a fourth-quarter touchdown.
The Tuscaloosa News | Dusty Compton

Far left: Alabama's Kareem Jackon (3) blocks a punt.
The Tuscaloosa News | Jason Harless

Left: Mississippi State's wide receiver is brought down by Alabama defenders Kareem Jackson (3) and Brandon Fanney (98) in the second quarter.
The Tuscaloosa News | Dusty Compton

Left: Alabama running back Glen Coffee (38) attempts to escape the grasp of Mississippi State defenders during the first quarter.
The Tuscaloosa News | Jason Harless

GAME STATS

UA VS. MISS. STATE | NOV. 15, 2008

Score by quarters	1	2	3	4	Final
Miss. State	0	7	0	0	7
Alabama	5	7	10	10	32

Team statistics	Ala.	MSU
First downs	17	9
— By rush	8	1
— By pass	9	6
— By penalty	0	2
Rushing attempts	48	22
Yds. gained rushing	208	55
Yds. lost rushing	10	20
Net yds. rushing	198	35
Passes attempted	19	28
Passes completed	12	11
Had intercepted	0	0
Net yds. passing	166	132
Total offensive plays	67	50
Total offense	364	167
Avg. gain per play	5.4	3.3
Fumbles-lost	2-0	2-1
Interceptions-yds.	0-0	0-0
Penalties-yds.	5-52	5-25
Punts-yards	5-215	10-374
Yards per punt	43.0	37.4
Punt returns-yds.	7-161	2-1
Kickoff returns-yds.	2-29	7-153
Possession	35:33	24:27
3rd-down conv.	6-14	2-12

AP Top 25

1. **Alabama (10-0)**
2. Texas Tech (10-0)
3. Florida (8-1)
4. Texas (9-1)
5. Oklahoma (9-1)
6. USC (8-1)
7. Penn State (9-1)
8. Utah (10-0)
9. Boise State (9-0)
10. Ohio State (8-2)
11. Oklahoma State (8-2)
12. Missouri (8-2)
13. Georgia (8-2)
14. Ball State (9-0)
15. TCU (9-2)
16. Brigham Young (9-1)
17. North Carolina (7-2)
18. Michigan State (9-2)
19. LSU (6-3)
20. Florida State (7-2)
21. Pittsburgh (7-2)
22. Cincinnati (7-2)
23. Oregon State (6-3)
24. South Carolina (7-2)
25. Tulsa (8-1)

BCS Top 10

1. **Alabama**
2. Texas Tech
3. Texas
4. Florida
5. Oklahoma
6. USC
7. Utah
8. Penn State
9. Boise State
10. Georgia

Left: Mark Ingram hoists the footb in celebration after scoring on a rur during the fourth quarter.
The Tuscaloosa News | Jason Harless

Above: Ingram outruns Mississipp State for a big gain during the third quarter. *The Tuscaloosa News | Jason Harless*

Top: Javier Arenas looks for running room on a 46-yard punt return durir the second quarter.
The Tuscaloosa News | Jason Harless

Above: Tight end Brad Smelley (17) dives for yardage after receiving a pass in the fourth quarter.
The Tuscaloosa News | Dusty Compton

Top right: Tight end Nick Walker (88) attempts to escape the grasp of Mississippi State defenders after a reception in the first quarter.
The Tuscaloosa News | Jason Harless

to Jamayel Smith — in one drive. (Those two completions accounted for 37 percent of MSU's total offense on the night.)

The touchdown gave MSU a 7-5 lead with 10:19 remaining in the half, but the Crimson Tide reeled off 27 unanswered points to pull away.

Arenas ignited the Crimson Tide later in the quarter with a 46-yard punt return to the MSU 2-yard line. Two plays later, John Parker Wilson scored on a quarterback sneak and UA never trailed again.

Wilson's touchdown snapped Alabama's long drought without an offensive touchdown against MSU, a barren period that reached back to the 2004 season. By the time Wilson went into the end zone with 4:47 remaining in the second quarter, the streak had covered 210 minutes and 41 seconds of football.

Arenas did even more in the third quarter. After MSU's first possession of the half stalled, he fielded a McAdams punt at the 20-yard line and, behind good blocking, went untouched down the right sideline for the 80-yard touchdown.

"The wall return is one of the prettiest plays in football, and that was a good one," Saban said.

Alabama added two more Tiffin field goals of 34 and 35 yards to push the lead to 25-7 with 11:14 remaining.

A 34-yard Wilson-to-Julio Jones completion set up the final Alabama score, with Mark Ingram going over from the 1-yard line with just under eight minutes to play.

The 11 wins recorded by the Crimson Tide on the season marked the most by an Alabama team since the 1994 Crimson Tide finished with a 12-1 record. ■

THE UNIVERSITY OF ALA
ALABAMA
ALABAMA

OPPONENT:

AUBURN

FINAL SCORE: ALABAMA 36 | AUBURN 0

Like his famous father before him, Leigh Tiffin has now kicked a field goal as the clock ticked down to 0:00, one that gave the University of Alabama football team all the points it needed to beat the Auburn Tigers.

Of course, this kick came at the end of the first quarter and the Crimson Tide added 33 points of icing on the cake, pounding Auburn, 36-0, to record its most lopsided victory in the in-state series in 46 years.

The victory ended Auburn's six-game winning streak in the rivalry, but, more importantly, capped an undefeated regular season for the Tide, giving Alabama a perfect record to match its No. 1 national ranking going into the Southeastern Conference Championship Game showdown with the Florida Gators.

Alabama's defense was so dominant, limiting Auburn to just 170 total yards, including just eight yards rushing in the second half, it felt likely that Tiffin's first-quarter field goal would probably hold up.

"It's sweet to be able to finish those guys off, especially after not being able to beat them so far," said Crimson Tide senior quarterback John Parker Wilson. "It's great to come out and finish.

"We were able to wear them down, the way we were running the ball, and we pretty much made them quit."

It all started in the trenches.

"We were able to control the line of scrimmage," said Tide head coach Nick

Above: Alabama's Eryk Anders (32) sacks Auburn quarterback Kodi Burns in the second quarter.
The Tuscaloosa News | Dusty Compton

Left: Bryant-Denny Stadium was sold out for this year's Iron Bowl. Alabama beat Auburn for the first time in seven years.
The Tuscaloosa News | Robert Sutton

AUBURN
MAZE
4

Above: Nick Saban walks the end zone prior to kickoff.
The Tuscaloosa News | Rober Sutton

Left: Alabama defenders drag Auburn running back Mario Fannin to the ground during a kick return in the third quarter. *The Tuscaloosa News | Dusty Compton*

Opposite page: Alabama's Marquis Maze (4) makes a 34-yard touchdown reception against Auburn defensive back Neiko Thorpe in the fourth quarter.
The Tuscaloosa News | Robert Sutton

Above: Glen Coffee (38) makes a 41-yard touchdown run in the second quarter. *The Tuscaloosa News | Dusty Compton*
Right: Alabama fans cheer on the Tide. *The Tuscaloosa News | Dusty Compton*
Top right: Alabama's Ali Sharrief breaks up a pass intended for Derek Winter in the first quarter. *The Tuscaloosa News | Dusty Compton*
Opposite page: Nathan Davis, center, and other decorated fans cheer on the Tide in Bryant-Denny Stadium. *The Tuscaloosa News | Dusty Compton*

Saban. "We were able to run it on them and they couldn't run it on us, and that put their quarterback in a position where he had to try to beat us in different ways."

None of those ways worked for Tiger quarterback Kodi Burns, who was 9 of 23 for 113 yards on a misty evening.

The game started as anticipated, a defensive struggle. It was more of a struggle for Alabama on its early possessions, thanks to a pair of deft Clinton Durst punts that pinned UA inside its 10-yard line.

On the second of those possessions, though, Alabama was able to power its way into Auburn territory. That drive culminated on a 37-yard field goal by Tiffin, but with the field position flipped, Auburn never really had the Tide in jeopardy again.

"When you are in that situation, you just talk about getting first downs," Wilson said. "You don't get too far ahead of yourselves. You get one, you get another and then you start moving. We just

got a field goal, but it was a big drive."

The next march started after a short Durst punt put Alabama at its 35. With better field position, Alabama scored on a four-play drive, capped by Glen Coffee's 41-yard run for the touchdown.

Auburn's deepest penetration and its only legitimate scoring chance came late in the first half. Burns scrambled for two solid gainers and the Tigers got to the Alabama 24 with five seconds remaining before halftime.

Tiger kicker Morgan Hull then booted the ball through the uprights — but not before the Tide bench had called time-out. On Hull's second attempt, his low kick was blocked by Bobby Greenwood, preserving Alabama's 10-0 lead.

In the second half, the gap widened significantly. Auburn contributed to its own problems with three turnovers, all

Top left: Glen Coffee gains part of his 144 rushing yards. *The Tuscaloosa News | Dan Lopez*
Above: Auburn head football coach Tommy Tuberville looks on in the second quarter.
The Tuscaloosa News | Dan Lopez
Left: Alabama receiver Nikita Stover (9) outruns Auburn defender Walter McFadden for a touchdown during the third quarter.
The Tuscaloosa News | Jason Harless
Opposite page: Alabama's Mark Ingram (22) is tackled while Earl Alexander (82) tries to block.
The Tuscaloosa News | Dan Lopez

GAME STATS

UA VS. AUBURN | NOV. 29, 2008

Score by quarters	1	2	3	4	Final
Auburn	0	0	0	0	0
Alabama	3	7	19	7	36

Team statistics	AU	Ala.
First downs	8	21
— By rush	4	13
— By pass	4	6
— By penalty	0	2
Rushing attempts	30	50
Yds. gained rushing	86	255
Yds. lost rushing	29	21
Net yds. rushing	57	234
Passes attempted	23	18
Passes completed	9	10
Had intercepted	0	0
Net yds. passing	113	178
Total offensive plays	53	68
Total offense	170	412
Avg. gain per play	3.2	6.1
Fumbles-lost	3-3	1-0
Interceptions-yds.	0-0	0-0
Penalties-yds.	4-45	1-4
Punts-yards	9-383	5-167
Yards per punt	42.6	33.4
Punt returns-yds.	2-19	2-20
Kickoff returns-yds.	7-122	0-0
Possession	24:23	35:37
3rd-down conv.	4-14	6-15

AP Top 25

1. **Alabama (11-0)**
2. Florida (10-1)
3. Oklahoma (10-1)
4. Texas (10-1)
5. USC (9-1)
6. Penn State (11-1)
7. Texas Tech (10-1)
8. Utah (12-0)
9. Boise State (11-0)
10. Ohio State (10-2)
11. Oklahoma State (9-2)
12. Missouri (9-2)
13. Georgia (9-2)
14. TCU (10-2)
15. Ball State (11-0)
16. Cincinnati (9-2)
17. Oregon State (8-3)
18. Georgia Tech (8-3)
19. Oregon (8-3)
20. Boston College (8-3)
21. Brigham Young (10-2)
22. Michigan State (9-3)
23. Florida State (8-3)
24. Northwestern (9-3)
25. Mississippi (7-4)

BCS Top 10

1. **Alabama**
2. Texas
3. Oklahoma
4. Florida
5. USC
6. Utah
7. Texas Tech
8. Penn State
9. Boise State
10. Ohio State

fumbles, but the Tigers were never able to move deeper than the Alabama 47-yard line as the Tide pulled away.

The first fumble, a Brad Lester bobble, put Alabama in business at the Tiger 39, and UA delivered the knockout punch on the ensuing play. Wilson rolled to the right and found fellow senior Nikita Stover behind the AU defense for a touchdown. Tiffin's PAT was blocked, but Alabama led, 16-0.

Three plays later, Burns bobbled a snap and the Crimson Tide's massive defensive lineman, Terrence Cody, recovered at the Auburn 45.

This time, the Tide's march was more methodical, but equally effective. Freshman Mark Ingram set Alabama up by taking a short pass from Wilson and gaining 27 yards to convert a third-and-14 situation. Five plays later, Ingram capped the drive with a 1-yard touchdown run.

After that, it was time to examine Auburn's luggage for hotel towels and complimentary soap because the Tigers had essentially checked out.

Alabama's next drive covered 50 yards, with Ingram ripping for the final 34 on three carries, including his second touchdown, a 14-yard run with 2:10 remaining. That capped a 19-point, third-quarter blitz by Alabama.

The fourth quarter was more of the same. Saban pulled his seniors on offense with seven minutes remaining, to thunderous applause. The Crimson Tide reserves were able to tack on one more touchdown on a 34-yard pass from backup quarterback Greg McElroy to freshman Marquis Maze with 2:49 remaining.

The 36-0 final was Alabama's first shutout of Auburn since 1992. It marked the first time the Tigers had been shut out by any opponent since Southern California blanked AU in the 2003 season opener.

"My emotions are through the roof," said Alabama safety Rashad Johnson. "I cannot really explain how it feels. We did it in a first-class manner with a shutout, and were able to dominate the game."

Auburn finished its season at 5-7, its first losing season since 1999, and head coach Tommy Tuberville signed a letter of resignation in the days following the game. ■

Above: Terrence Cody (62) celebrates after a fumble recovery in the third quarter. *The Tuscaloosa News | Dusty Compton*

Opposite page: Alabama preserves the shutout victory over Auburn as Bobby Greenwood blocks a field-goal attempt. *The Tuscaloosa News | Dan Lopez*

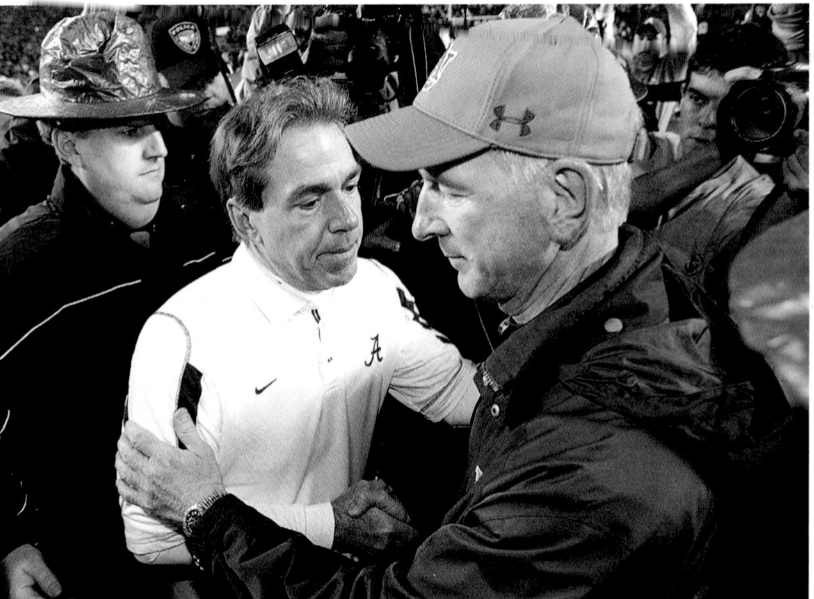

Left: Alabama fans celebrate after the game, with the final score in the background.
The Tuscaloosa News | Dan Lopez

Top: Coaches Nick Saban, left, and Tommy Tuberville meet at midfield after the Tide's victory. *The Tuscaloosa News | Dusty Compton*

Above: Bryant-Denny Stadium lights up with crimson and white.
The Tuscaloosa News | Robert Sutton

Opposite page: Defensive back Marquis Johnson (24) celebrates the Tide's victory.
The Tuscaloosa News | Dan Lopez

INSIDE THE GAME

It was over long before it was over.

The top-ranked University of Alabama football team knew the six-game losing streak to rival Auburn had come to an end before the third quarter was finished. Somewhere along the way to a shutout victory in Bryant-Denny Stadium, it became clear that this game belonged to the Crimson Tide, and the players on the field sensed it.

About the time Mark Ingram scored on a 1-yard run midway through the third quarter to push Alabama's lead to 22 points, any lingering doubt was erased. Not long after, the Tide took complete command of the game — and knew it.

"We were just pounding them, and they weren't stopping us at all," junior linebacker Cory Reamer said. "You could tell they were starting to give up.

"It's something that was fun to be a part of. We didn't want it to end. We were enjoying the moment."

That moment carried through a fourth quarter that saw head coach Nick Saban gradually remove key starters from the game, with seniors like Antoine Caldwell, John Parker Wilson and Bobby Greenwood leaving to standing ovations from a packed-out crowd of 92,138.

"It really was special to get to come off in the middle of a (drive) like that and just have everybody cheering," Wilson said. "My last play, it's special to me."

For Wilson and his teammates, it was all the more special because the perfect regular season was punctuated by a decisive victory over Alabama's cross-state rival.

"It's a good way to go out," the quarterback said. "We beat them good and left no doubt."

After the final seconds ticked off the game clock, Alabama players trotted onto the field and celebrated while Saban took a victory lap around the stadium to acknowledge Alabama fans.

"I was thanking them," Saban said. "I was thanking our fans for their support, I was thanking our fans for the atmosphere that they create and I was thanking our fans for the positive energy that has affected our program in a positive way."

Alabama players made their way to the locker room for their own private celebration. They prayed and sang the "Yea Alabama" fight song together.

"They were pretty excited," Saban said. "It's a pretty unique three or four minutes. It's great to be a part of."

This locker room celebration was one Tide players will remember for a long time.

"Especially tonight, we congratulated the seniors for all the hard work they've put in," Reamer said. "Everybody was pretty excited. Everybody was having a lot more fun after this one. It being the last regular-season game and us beating Auburn the way we did and dominating the way we did out on the field, you get a little more pumped up about it."

Saban's message to the team was simple: "That I was proud of them and that it was a great win and they made a lot of people proud. It's great accomplishment for them to get where they are right now. They did it with a lot of hard work and perseverance and commitment, and really kind of did it the hard way."

Saban joined in the celebration. "I was happy and dancing in the locker room," he said.

Senior safety Rashad Johnson wasn't so sure.

"Coach Saban, I didn't see him dancing," the Sulligent native said. "He might have been. I want to get that on YouTube."

And while the SEC Championship Game showdown with Florida loomed, for one day Alabama players were able to bask in the thrill of finally beating Auburn.

"It's one of the most fulfilling feelings I've had since I've been in college," junior offensive lineman Mike Johnson said. "To finish the season 12-0, the regular season, and to beat your rival like that at home, you couldn't ask for a better feeling." ■

TIME OUT WITH #14 JOHN PARKER WILSON

John Parker Wilson will leave the University of Alabama as the school's all-time leading passer.

In fact, he has thrown for more yards, thrown more touchdown passes, thrown more completions, thrown more passes period and even taken more snaps than any quarterback in Crimson Tide history.

That's more than Joe Namath or Kenny Stabler or Harry Gilmer or Bart Starr, to name a few.

For all that, the legacy of the senior from Hoover going into his final season at the Capstone was centered around the number 13. He had won 13 games as a starter and lost 13.

Now the 6-foot-2, 211-pound Wilson — who wore jersey No. 14 — will instead be remembered as the player who led Alabama to 13 straight victories, starting with the final game of his junior season.

Wilson redeemed his legacy by guiding Alabama to a perfect 12-0 regular season. Instead of being remembered for turnovers that cost the Crimson Tide games against Florida State, LSU and Mississippi State his junior year, he will now be hailed as the leader who guided Alabama to an overtime victory at LSU and ended Auburn's six-game winning streak over the Tide, and for his part in impressive road victories at Georgia and Tennessee in his final season as the Tide's signal-caller.

How did Wilson transform himself into a top-notch game manager who was a finalist for the Johnny Unitas Golden Arm Award and a semifinalist for the Davey O'Brien Award? He didn't strong-arm his way to better play. Instead, he mastered the mental part of the game.

Left: John Parker Wilson prepares to pass during the Arkansas State game.
The Tuscaloosa News | Robert Sutton

Below: Wilson prepares to deliver a pass downfield to Marquis Maze for an Alabama touchdown as Ole Miss defenders put on the pressure.
The Tuscaloosa News | Jason Harless

Opposite page: Wilson passes the ball in the second half of the SEC Championship Game against the Florida Gators in Atlanta.
The Tuscaloosa News | Robert Sutton

"I just work on making good decisions," Wilson said.

Wilson benefited from a less complex offense installed by Jim McElwain, Alabama's new offensive coordinator for the 2008 season, from a strong running game and from one of the nation's best offensive lines.

He also matured into the job, drawing on the experiences of two previous seasons as a starter.

Head coach Nick Saban watched Wilson's growth process.

"To be able to kind of stay in his zone and make business decisions has probably been the biggest difference in his play," the coach said.

Wilson cut down on his turnovers and became a master of the simple art of throwing the ball away to avoid a bad play. Mostly, he learned to let the game come to him.

When he was called upon to make plays in the passing game against Georgia and Tennessee and LSU, he proved himself capable. When the running game was in complete command against Clemson and Arkansas and Auburn, Wilson was content to play caretaker.

"I think my decision-making has been a lot better," he said, "keeping our team in good plays and in position to win."

Winning, ultimately, was what Wilson did best, and that will be his Alabama legacy. ■

OPPONENT:

FLORIDA

SEC CHAMPIONSHIP

FINAL SCORE: ALABAMA 20 | FLORIDA 31

All that stood between the University of Alabama football team and a chance to play for a national championship was 15 minutes — and Tim Tebow. That proved to be too much.

Alabama took a three-point lead into the fourth quarter of the Southeastern Conference Championship Game in the Georgia Dome, but watched its grasp on greatness slip away as Florida pulled away for a 31-20 victory, the first loss of the year for the Crimson Tide.

The game matched a No. 1-ranked Alabama team against No. 2 Florida, with national championship implications. The victory put Florida in the BCS title game against Oklahoma, as well as giving the Gators the SEC title.

Alabama accepted a trip to New Orleans to play Utah in the Sugar Bowl while wondering what might have been.

As in any classic game — and the contest did live up to most, if not all, of the pregame hyperbole — every moment, from Florida's opening touchdown drive to John Parker Wilson's late, coffin-closing interception, resonated in some way.

But no sequence was more important than Florida's go-ahead drive in the fourth quarter.

"I don't know the entire history of Florida football, but I can imagine that drive going down as one of the greatest ever," said Florida coach Urban Meyer.

The Crimson Tide had just taken the lead by powering the football down the field on an impressive 65-yard drive, or, as Meyer described

Above: John Parker Wilson (14) is pressured by Florida defenders in the second quarter. *The Tuscaloosa News | Dusty Compton*
Left: Mark Ingram (22) makes his way over the goal line for a third-quarter touchdown. *The Tuscaloosa News | Dusty Compton*

Above: The team participates in a pre-game practice at the Georgia Dome. *The Tuscaloosa News | Dusty Compton*
Top right: Alabama quarterback John Parker Wilson practices the day before the game. *The Tuscaloosa News | Dusty Compton*
Right: Players run through plays. *The Tuscaloosa News | Dusty Compton*
Far right: Coach Nick Saban talks to members of the media during a pregame press conference. *The Tuscaloosa News | Dusty Compton*
Opposite page: Florida's quarterback Tim Tebow is gang tackled by the Alabama defense during a third-and-short in the first quarter. *The Tuscaloosa News | Jason Harless*

it, "jamming it down our throats." But the drive ended not in a touchdown, but in a 27-yard Leigh Tiffin field goal, putting the Crimson Tide ahead 20-17.

"I thought that would have been a big momentum thing right there, if we had scored a touchdown instead of a field goal," Crimson Tide coach Nick Saban said.

Still, Alabama had taken the lead. Florida started its answering drive in good field position after Brandon James — a weapon for the Gators all day long — returned the UA kickoff to the 37-yard line. The Gators moved into Alabama territory and, on a crucial third-and-three, appeared to have been stopped short of a first down at the Crimson Tide 43-yard line.

UA freshman linebacker Dont'a Hightower, however, was flagged for a face-mask violation, putting the Gators at the Crimson Tide 28. Five plays later, Jeffery Demps scored from the 1-yard line to give Florida a lead it never relinquished.

Alabama's ensuing possession went three-and-out. Florida's answering drive pushed the Tide's stalling from "critical" to "decisive." Powered by Tebow, the game's MVP, Florida marched 65 yards and scored again. Tebow hit a 33-yard pass to Louis Murphy to flip field position, then — after a penalty on the UF sidelines pushed the Gators back from the 1-yard line — the 2007 Heisman Trophy winner threw a 6-yard strike to Riley Cooper to put UF ahead, 31-20.

The Crimson Tide's last-gasp drive ended when Wilson threw an interception that ended all Alabama hopes with 99 seconds to play.

Tebow finished the game with 57 yards rushing and was 14 of 22 passing for 216 yards.

"He's a great competitor, no doubt," Saban said. "I think he takes his team on

Above: Alabama's Javier Arenas (28) makes a return in the fourth quarter.
The Tuscaloosa News | Robert Sutton

Left: Florida quarterback Tim Tebow is brought down by Alabama defenders Brandon Deaderick (95) and Brandon Fanney (98) in the third quarter.
The Tuscaloosa News | Dusty Compton

79
41
SEC

Left: Florida defenders fight Julio Jones (8) for a pass in the fourth quarter. *The Tuscaloosa News | Dusty Compton*
Above: Alabama defenders react after a Florida touchdown in the first quarter. *The Tuscaloosa News | Dusty Compton*
Top right: Alabama's Justin Woodall (27) cuts the legs out from under a Florida running back in the second quarter.
The Tuscaloosa News | Jason Harless
Opposite page: Glen Coffee (38) breaks the tackle of a Florida defender on a touchdown run during the first quarter.
The Tuscaloosa News | Jason Harless

GAME STATS

UA VS. FLORIDA | DEC. 6, 2008

Score by quarters	1	2	3	4	Final
Alabama	10	0	10	0	20
Florida	7	10	0	14	31

Team statistics	**Ala.**	**Fla.**
First downs	18	19
— By rush	11	9
— By pass	7	8
— By penalty	0	2
Rushing attempts	33	42
Yds. gained rushing	147	151
Yds. lost rushing	11	9
Net yds. rushing	136	142
Passes attempted	25	22
Passes completed	12	14
Had intercepted	1	0
Net yds. passing	187	216
Total offensive plays	58	64
Total offense	323	358
Avg. gain per play	5.6	5.6
Fumbles-lost	0-0	0-0
Interceptions-yds.	0-0	1-24
Penalties-yds.	2-31	6-45
Punts-yards	4-164	3-143
Yards per punt	41.0	47.7
Punt returns-yds.	2-20	3-25
Kickoff returns-yds.	4-95	5-121
Possession time	27:56	32:04
3rd-down conv.	5-12	7-13

AP Top 25

1. **Alabama (12-0)**
2. Florida (11-1)
3. Texas (11-1)
4. Oklahoma (11-1)
5. USC (10-1)
6. Penn State (11-1)
7. Utah (12-0)
8. Texas Tech (11-1)
9. Boise State (12-0)
10. Ohio State (10-2)
11. TCU (10-2)
12. Ball State (12-0)
13. Cincinnati (10-2)
14. Oklahoma State (9-3)
15. Georgia Tech (9-3)
16. Oregon (9-3)
17. Georgia (9-3)
18. Boston College (9-3)
19. Missouri (9-3)
20. Brigham Young (10-2)
21. Michigan State (9-3)
22. Mississippi (8-4)
23. Pittsburgh (8-3)
24. Northwestern (9-3)
25. Oregon State (8-4)

BCS Top 10

1. **Alabama**
2. Oklahoma
3. Texas
4. Florida
5. USC
6. Utah
7. Texas Tech
8. Penn State
9. Boise State
10. Ohio State

Left: Alabama's Rolando McClain (25) tackles a Florida Gator. *The Tuscaloosa News | Robert Sutton*

Below: Alabama's Darius Hanks (15) reaches for the ball in the second quarter. *The Tuscaloosa News | Robert Sutton*

Above: Julio Jones (8) reaches high for a pass in the second quarter.
The Tuscaloosa News | Dusty Compton

his shoulders a lot. I think his leadership really affects his teammates."

Florida, a 10-point favorite, looked the part in the first quarter, stopping Alabama on the first possession, then driving 59 yards to take a 7-0 lead on the first of Tebow's three touchdown passes, a 3-yard toss to Carl Moore.

Alabama came back with a lightning drive that consisted off a 64-yard Wilson-to-Julio Jones pass, followed by an 18-yard touchdown run by Glen Coffee. Despite nagging injuries, Coffee rushed for [illegible] yards on 21 carries in the game.

Alabama got a 30-yard Tiffin field goal later in the quarter to take a 10-7 lead.

Two special-teams miscues by Alabama helped set up a pair of second-quarter Gator scores.

First, a fake field goal after Alabama had reached the Gators' 32-yard line, a play that Saban later said "should not have been run" due to Florida's formation, found no success.

Florida took over and marched for a game-tying field goal.

Then, on the ensuing kickoff, Javier Arenas fielded the ball and stepped out of bounds at the 4-yard line. The Crimson Tide quickly punted the ball back, and Florida drove 57 yards for a touchdown — a 5-yard pass from Tebow to David Nelson — that gave UF a 17-10 halftime lead.

Alabama tied the game on Mark Ingram's 2-yard touchdown run with 8:32 remaining in the third quarter, then went ahead on Tiffin's field goal with eight seconds remaining in the period.

But the fourth quarter belonged to Florida.

Saban congratulated Florida, but added that he was "proud of what our football team accomplished this year.

"We didn't get the result that we hoped for today. We kind of ran out of gas in the fourth quarter. But I think both teams played extremely well in this game." ■

Gators

Above: Nick Saban talks with Florida coach Urban Meyer after the game. *The Tuscaloosa News | Jason Harless* **Right:** Saban leaves the Georgia Dome after the game. *The Tuscaloosa News | Dusty Compton* **Opposite page:** Julio Jones (98) attempts to escape a Florida defender during the first quarter. *The Tuscaloosa News | Jason Harless*

INSIDE THE GAME

Julio Jones didn't have a lot to say after the Southeastern Conference Championship Game.

The Alabama Crimson Tide's freshman receiver did most of his talking on the field.

"It speaks for itself," junior cornerback Javier Arenas said. "Exciting to watch. He's a physical receiver. I love going against him in practice.

"You all see it, watch it. He's great."

By finishing with 124 receiving yards on five catches, Jones recorded his third 100-yard performance of the season, and with junior running back Glen Coffee became just the third teammates in the history of the SEC title game to have 100-yard rushing and receiving performances.

Alabama's Derrick Lassic and David Palmer did the same trick in 1992.

"He's probably going to be the best ever at Alabama at wide receiver," junior left tackle Andre Smith said.

Two plays by Jones stood out in particular.

After Florida scored a touchdown on its opening possession, it was Jones' 64-yard reception — with cornerback Joe Haden missing a tackle and Jones faking his way by another defensive back — that swung the momentum back to Alabama. Coffee scored on the following play to tie the game.

It was not only Alabama's longest pass play of the game, but the season.

"It was a routine catch," Jones said. "I do it all the time in practice."

His other key reception came on Alabama's first possession of the second half, when the Tide had third-and-seven at its own 9. He made an outstanding adjustment to reach up and snare the ball for an 18-yard sideline reception and prevent UA from having to punt from its own end zone.

The Crimson Tide offense went 91 yards on 15 plays to tie the game at 17.

All of Jones' receptions came on scoring drives.

"I think I did OK," he said. "I can get better."

A number of other true freshmen made significant contributions for Alabama, both against Florida and on the season as a whole.

Even though he was limited to 21 rushing yards on eight carries against UF, running back Mark Ingram scored his 12th touchdown on a 2-yard run. Not only is that an Alabama freshman record, but it is also tied for the eighth-most in program history.

"It was a good year," Ingram said. "I learned a lot from these 12 games."

Although his production decreased during the stretch run, which can be common for players enduring their first collegiate season, Ingram still finished among the conference rushing leaders with 717 yards on 135 carries through the title game.

Ingram, like Jones, was part of a heralded No. 1-ranked recruiting class. Overall, Alabama played 16 true freshman this season, third-most in the country behind Miami and Florida.

"We just came in with the attitude that we were going to turn the program around," Ingram, said. "A lot of us played. A lot of us played major roles. A lot of us played minor roles.

"These seniors had a lot to do with it. They taught us a lot." ■

ONE WAY

75TH ANNUAL

SUGAR BOWL

FINAL SCORE: ALABAMA 17 | UTAH 31

THE SCENE

Snappy jazz and soulful blues filtered through the air. The scent of Cajun spices and Creole sauces wafted over the streets through restaurant doors. Colorful signs and pushy doormen competed to attract customers into bars and curio shops.

The sights and sounds of the French Quarter were the same as always, but there was something different, something that hadn't been seen here for 16 years: Alabama fans were back for the Sugar Bowl.

Not since the end of the 1992 season had Crimson Tide supporters arrived en masse in New Orleans, but by New Year's Eve it was becoming obvious that Alabama was back.

They came to eat and drink and party. And, of course, attend a football game.

But first, there was plenty to do and see.

"Cheap alcohol, good-looking women and stuff that's not allowed in Alabama," said Scott Knox, a Tuscaloosa County High School graduate.

The 34-year-old Birmingham resident was taking in the scene with a rum-and-coke in hand 30 minutes after he arrived.

"I checked into the hotel and walked to Bourbon Street," he said.

Knox saw Alabama's army of supporters on his way to the Big Easy.

"We stopped twice on the way down, and both the gas station and Chic-fil-A were full of Alabama fans," he said. "There were flags and stickers everywhere."

Above: UA football fans cheer from the balcony of the Bourbon Street Blues Company on Bourbon Street in the French Quarter on New Year's Eve. *The Tuscaloosa News | Dan Lopez*

Left: Alabama fans, Utah fans and visitors revel just after midnight on Jan. 1, 2009, on Bourbon Street. *The Tuscaloosa News | Dan Lopez*

Left: Alabama fans walk down Bourbon Street on New Year's Eve. *The Tuscaloosa News | Dan Lopez*
Far left: An Alabama flag flies over a busy street in the French Quarter.
The Tuscaloosa News | Dan Lopez
Below: The French Quarter just past the stroke of midnight on Jan. 1, 2009, is packed with visitors.
The Tuscaloosa News | Dan Lopez

Crimson Tide players also took in the city's sites. They attended a New Orleans Saints game and got loudly booed by LSU fans when they were introduced at a New Orleans Hornets NBA contest. Some went on a "ghost tour" of allegedly haunted houses, while others sampled the cuisine.

"I had a little alligator," senior tight end Travis McCall said. "It was pretty good."

Mostly, when they weren't practicing Alabama players wandered the French Quarter and took in the ambiance that makes it so unique.

Top and center right : Nick Saban and UA players hand out signed hats as they visited some of the young patients at Children's Hospital in New Orleans on Dec. 30. *The Tuscaloosa News | Dan Lopez*

Below: Saban, left, and Utah head football coach Kyle Whittingham attend a pregame press conference. *The Tuscaloosa News | Dan Lopez*

Bottom: The Louisiana Superdome against the New Orleans skyline. *The Tuscaloosa News | Dan Lopez*

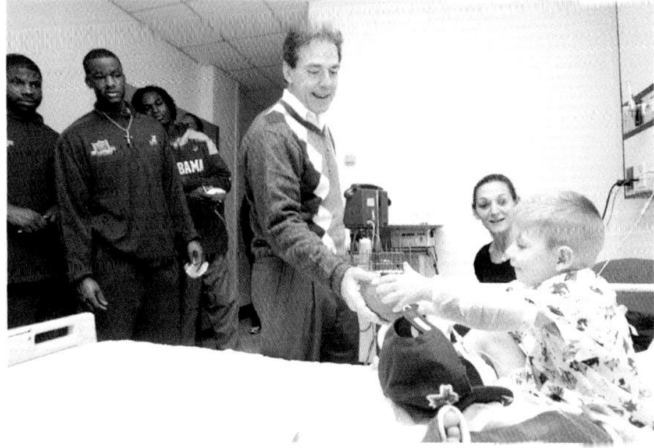

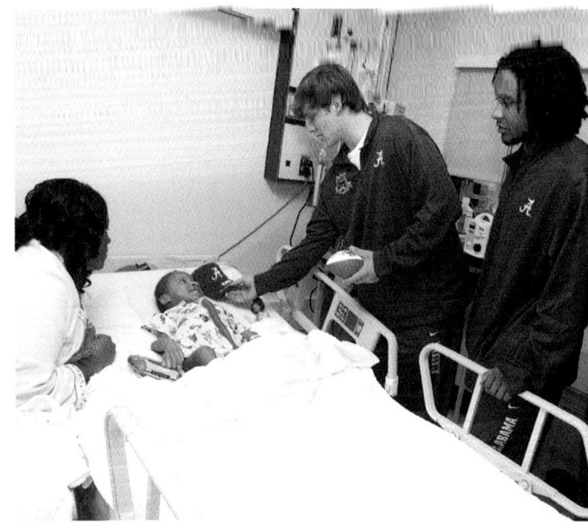

"On Bourbon Street, this dude had like a Zorro outfit on, walking by himself with a hand grenade (drink)," Javier Arenas said. "That was odd. You don't see that."

The impact of Crimson Tide fans wasn't lost on the local economy. Bourbon Street Blues Co. had Kid Rock's "All Summer Long," which borrows heavily from "Sweet Home Alabama," blaring at full volume on a regular basis.

"Every time we play it, people come in," said Steve Hood, the club's 40-year-old emcee.

Hood noticed a distinct pattern among the bar's patrons as the game approached.

"All Alabama, no Utah," he said. "Alabama fans are amazing."

Just down the street at Lipstixx, A Gentleman's Club, street barker Jason Thompson confirmed the same thing.

"Alabama fans are fun," he said. "They might be a little more boisterous. I don't know about Utah people. I haven't seen many of them, but Alabama people are great."

Not all Tide fans flocked to Bourbon Street right away. Bill Gray, a 50-year-old Mobile native, flew all the way from his home on Waikiki Beach in Hawaii and quickly migrated to another of the city's famous attractions.

"I've been to New Orleans off and on all my life," he said. "One of the things you must do in New Orleans is go to Café Du Monde and have beignets and coffee with chicory."

Across Jackson Square from the famous French-style donut shop, in front of St. Louis Cathedral, a 12-member band of street musicians equipped with a tuba and trumpets and trombones played as Alabama fan Carolyn Eades of Ramsey, N.J., clapped along.

"I can't believe I'm going to the Sugar Bowl," she said. "This is a first. We're going to watch Alabama win."

Rick Crawford, a 45-year-old plumber from Fort Oglethorpe, Ga., who came to root for the Tide, noticed others wearing Alabama shirts everywhere he went.

"It's like a home game," he said.

Gray, the fan from Hawaii, watched the numbers of UA supporters on the streets grow by the hour.

"It's Alabama season," he said. "We've been walking around and it's been 'Roll Tide' everywhere.

"It's the Sugar Bowl. It's Alabama. We're back." ■

THE GAME

All season long, the University of Alabama football team had a simple slogan — "Finish."

In the Sugar Bowl, the Crimson Tide didn't finish in large part because it never really got started. Utah jumped out to a three-touchdown lead at the Louisiana Superdome, weathered a mid-game run by Alabama and pulled away for a 31-17 victory that capped an unbeaten season for the Utes and ended the Crimson Tide's year at 12-2.

"I'm responsible for having [the team] ready to play," Crimson Tide head coach Nick Saban said. "I don't think we were ready to play today, and I don't know why.

"We got down 21-0 and I was proud of our players for coming back to make it 21-17," Saban said. "But it was a horrible start, and we couldn't overcome it."

The first quarter was an unstinting parade of mis cues for the Crimson Tide, which misfired on

Above: Alabama running back Glen Coffee (38) picks up yards after escaping Utah defenders during the first quarter. *The Tuscaloosa News | Jason Harless*
Left: Alabama fans look on as Utah pulls ahead in the first quarter. *The Tuscaloosa News | Dusty Compton*
Far left: Wide receiver Julio Jones misses a reception during the first quarter. *The Tuscaloosa News | Dan Lopez*
Opposite page: Alabama's Javier Arenas (28) returns a punt for an Alabama touchdown as Utah punter Louie Sakoda (37) attempts to make the tackle during the second quarter. *The Tuscaloosa News | Jason Harless*

Above: Utah defensive back Sean Smith (4) breaks up a pass to Alabamas wide receiver Nikita Stover (9) in the second quarter.
The Tuscaloosa News | Dusty Compton

Left: Javier Arenas is congratulated by Nick Saban after a touchdown in the second quarter.
The Tuscaloosa News | Dan Lopez

Far left: Rashad Johnson, right, tackles Utah wide receiver Freddie Brown (88) during the second quarter.
The Tuscaloosa News | Dan Lopez

Above: Utah defender Greg Newman (56) tries to take down Alabama running back Mark Ingram (22) during a second quarter drive. *The Tuscaloosa News | Dusty Compton*

offense and appeared lost at times on defense. The first Crimson Tide drive was scuttled by a dropped pass. The second march saw Wilson throw an interception. The third drive ended with Wilson being sacked at the Crimson Tide 30.

After each of the failed marches, the Utes responded with touchdowns. Utah quarterback Brian Johnson hit five consecutive passes on the first march to move the Utes 68 yards for a score. The second drive ended when Matt Asiata took a direct snap and scored on a 2-yard run. The third march culminated with an 18-yard pass from Johnson to Bradon Godfrey, giving Utah a 21-0 lead in less than 11 minutes.

Alabama regrouped after that, although the

Above: John Parker Wilson throws a pass during the third quarter. *The Tuscaloosa News | Dan Lopez*
Right: Alabama's Julio Jones (8) misses a pass while being covered by Utah's Sean Smith (4) in the third quarter. *The Tuscaloosa News | Dusty Compton*

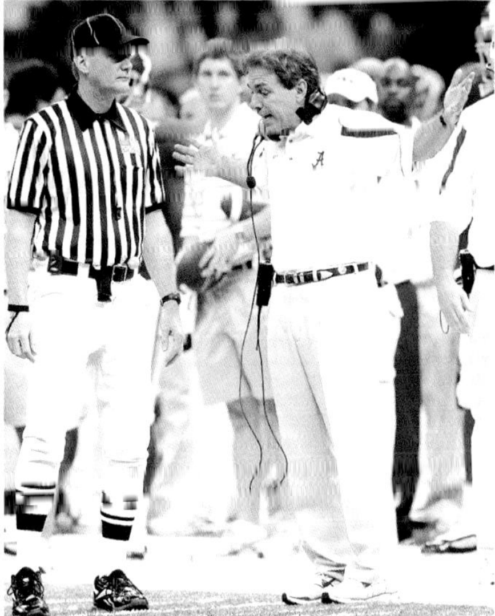

Above: Glen Coffee (38) moves the ball upfield while being covered by Utah's Mike Wright (20) in the third quarter.
The Tuscaloosa News | Dusty Compton

Top right: Nick Saban reacts to a call during the fourth quarter.
The Tuscaloosa News | Jason Harless

Left: Alabama lineman Bobby Greenwood (93) picks up a Utah fumble in the third quarter.
The Tuscaloosa News | Dusty Compton

Crimson Tide still looked inefficient on offense, a situation made no better when Mike Johnson injured an ankle, taking a second All-Southeastern Conference performer off the UA offensive line. The results of his absence and the more notable suspension of Outland Trophy winner Andre Smith were obvious: Utah sacked Wilson four times in the half and pressured him heavily on several other plays.

But Utah managed just 50 yards of offense over the next 19 minutes and Alabama crept closer thanks to special teams play, getting a 52-yard Leigh Tiffin field goal on the first play of the second quarter and adding a 73-yard Javier Arenas punt return to cut the lead to 21-10.

But the UA offense moved into Utah territory twice more and scored no points. Tiffin missed a 47-yard field-goal try after a sack of Wilson pushed the ball back eight yards on third down with 6:42 remaining in the half. Alabama was back in Utah territory when time expired in the first half, but hurt its chances with a holding penalty.

The Crimson Tide's biggest break of the game came on the first possession of the third quarter. Johnson fumbled, senior defensive lineman Bobby Greenwood recovered at the Ute 35 and Alabama went on to capitalize as Wilson capped the seven-play march with a 4-yard touchdown pass to Glen Coffee.

That score put Alabama back into the game, trailing 21-17 with most of the second half remaining.

But the Crimson Tide's offensive woes continued and two critical missed tackles allowed Utah to tack on an insurance touchdown. The score came on 28-yard pass from Johnson, the game's MVP, to David Reed, who broke Kareem Jackson's tackle and went into the end zone.

"One of the things that hurts you in bowl games, if you don't concentrate and

Above: John Parker Wilson (14), right, turns to run upfield as offensive lineman Marlon Davis's helmet comes off in the third quarter.
The Tuscaloosa News | Dusty Compton

Left: Javier Arenas (28) slips by Utah's Clint Mower (39) in the fourth quarter. *The Tuscaloosa News | Dan Lopez*
Below: Utah fans hold up a poster as fans cheer. *The Tuscaloosa News | Dan Lopez*
Bottom: A UA fan reacts during the fourth quarter. *The Tuscaloosa News | Dan Lopez*

get yourself in position to tackle is missed tackles," Saban said. "That hurt us badly. On their last (touchdown) drive, two missed tackles were two big plays that led to a touchdown."

"That was the difference tonight," said Alabama safety Rashad Johnson. "We tackled in practice every day, but I don't know why it didn't carry over into the bowl."

A Wilson sack and fumble in the final five minutes set up Utah's final points, a 28-yard field goal by All-American kicker Louie Sakoda.

"This is a great football team, a great group of guys," said Utah coach Kyle Whittingham.

Brian Johnson, who Saban called the "best system quarterback we have played all year," completed 27 of 41 passes for 336 yards and three touchdowns to earn the MVP accolade. Utah rushed for just 13 yards, but limited Alabama to just 31 yards on the ground. ■

Above: A Utah fan, right, celebrates next to disappointed Alabama fans in the final minutes of the fourth quarter. *The Tuscaloosa News | Dan Lopez*

Above: Members of the Alabama defensive unit look on during the final minutes of Alabama's 31-17 defeat. *The Tuscaloosa News | Jason Harless*

GAME STATS

UA VS. UTAH | JAN. 2, 2009

Score by quarters	1	2	3	4	Final
Utah	21	0	7	3	31
Alabama	0	10	7	0	17

Team statistics	Utah	Ala.
First downs	22	15
— By rush	3	5
— By pass	17	8
— By penalty	2	2
Rushing attempts	24	33
Yds. gained rushing	51	88
Yds. lost rushing	38	57
Net yds. rushing	13	31
Passes attempted	41	30
Passes completed	27	18
Had intercepted	0	2
Net yds. passing	336	117
Total offensive plays	65	63
Total offense	349	208
Avg. gain per play	5.4	3.3
Fumbles-lost	3-1	1-1
Interceptions-yds.	2-7	0-0
Penalties-yds.	10-91	7-67
Punts-yards	6-271	4-166
Yards per punt	45.2	41.5
Punt returns-yds.	1-2	1-73
Kickoff returns-yds.	4-93	6-149
Possession	28:42	31:18
3rd-down conv.	6-14	4-13

AP Top 25

1. Florida 12-1
2. Oklahoma 12-1
3. Texas 11-1
4. **Alabama 12-1**
5. Southern Cal 11-1
6. Penn State 11-1
7. Utah 12-0
8. Texas Tech 11-1
9. Boise State 12-0
10. Ohio State 10-2
11. TCU 10-2
12. Cincinnati 11-2
13. Oklahoma State 9-3
14. Georgia Tech 9-3
15. Oregon 9-3
16. Georgia 9-3
17. Brigham Young 10-2
18. Pittsburgh 9-3
19. Michigan State 9-3
20. Ole Miss 8-4
21. Virginia Tech 9-4
22. Northwestern 9-3
23. Ball State 12-1
24. Oregon State 8-4
25. Missouri 9-4

BCS Top 10

1. Oklahoma
2. Florida
3. Texas
4. **Alabama**
5. Southern Cal
6. Utah
7. Texas Tech
8. Penn State
9. Boise State
10. Ohio State

Above: Coach Nick Saban leaves the field at the Superdome after the game. *The Tuscaloosa News | Jason Harless*

Above: Quarterback John Parker Wilson, left, and wide receiver B.J. Scott leave the Superdome after the disappointing loss to Utah.
The Tuscaloosa News | Dan Lopez

Right: Terrence Cody, far right, reacts to the score during the final minutes of the game.
The Tuscaloosa News | Dan Lopez

INSIDE THE GAME

Freshman running back Mark Ingram could only shake his head as he walked off the field at the Louisiana Superdome. Linebacker Rolando McClain didn't even wait for the final seconds to tick off the clock before jogging to the locker room.

The University of Alabama fell behind by three touchdowns before the Sugar Bowl was 11 minutes old, but still didn't have enough time for a 31-17 defeat to the unheralded Utah Utes to fully sink in by the game's end.

"It's a real big shocker for us all," defensive lineman Terrence Cody said. "Everybody is real shocked."

Fourth-ranked Alabama went from the heights of a perfect 12-0 regular season to ending the 2008 campaign with back-to-back losses, falling to Florida in the Southeastern Conference Championship Game and then losing to 10-point underdog Utah, which came into the bowl ranked No. 7.

"Definitely not how I expected it to end," Crimson Tide defensive end Lorenzo Washington said. "I was never thinking about losing at all.

"Personally, this hurts. It turns a lot. I wanted to do it most of all for the seniors. This is one of the best Alabama teams in a while. I'm just sorry how it ended."

Alabama seemed to recover after allowing Utah to take a 21-0 lead in the first quarter, but never overtook the undefeated Utes.

"We had a game plan," Ingram said, "but we didn't execute."

Alabama players came into the game saying they respected Utah. After being outplayed in every facet of the game, they weren't so sure.

"I felt like as a team we may not have given them their due respect," running back Glen Coffee said. "As a football team, that is something that we should never let happen."

Alabama players were left to wonder whether the Sugar Bowl defeat would tarnish the legacy of a team that was perfect in the regular season.

"A little bit, yes, it does," Cody said. "But then no, because we still went undefeated.

"This doesn't take away our pride and dignity we had the whole season."

Defensive lineman Bobby Greenwood and eight other scholarship seniors ended their Alabama careers in defeat.

"I gave it my all out there," Greenwood said. "I can look at myself in the mirror and tell myself that. I'm definitely going to remember this the rest of my life.

"This is the end of my career and we came up short. All this program can do is build from this and take it into next year." ■

AFTERWARD

Leave it to Nick Saban to sum up the University of Alabama's 2008 football season.

When collecting one of his many national coach of the year awards, the Crimson Tide's head coach captured in words the magic that was made by Alabama on the football field in an unexpectedly rewarding season.

"This should be," Saban declared, "the team of the year award."

Indeed, that is just what the Crimson Tide became over the course of an undefeated regular season.

Alabama rose from a No. 24 preseason ranking to be ranked No. 1 for the first time since 1980. A team that was picked to finish in the middle of the pack in the Southeastern Conference Western Division race played its way to the SEC title game and came within a quarter of playing for the national title.

Along the way, the Crimson Tide exacted revenge on the likes of Georgia, LSU and Mississippi State, capping it off with a victory over cross-state rival Auburn. Alabama also humbled Clemson, manhandled Tennessee and dominated Arkansas.

Solid seniors like John Parker Wilson, Antoine Caldwell and Rashad Johnson blended with newcomers like Julio Jones, Terrence Cody and others from a recruiting class that had been ranked as the best in the nation. The result was a cohesive unit that was better than the sum of its parts.

As it happened, Alabama's season unraveled in the stretch run. The Crimson Tide took Florida into the final quarter in the SEC title game with a chance to play for the national title in the balance, but suffered its first defeat.

And with All-America tackle Andre Smith suspended in the days before the Sugar Bowl, Alabama wasn't able to regain its perfect regular-season form at the Louisiana Superdome in a surprising upset loss to Utah to close out the season.

It all begs the question of how the 2008 season will be remembered.

The finish was disappointing to an Alabama program that seemed poised to add a 13th national title to the trophy case, but the season will ultimately be remembered as a special one. This was a blue-collar team that won as much because of its work ethic as its talent, a group that exceeded all expectations.

The 2008 Crimson Tide's legacy, despite the finish, will be as the squad that for 12 games through the regular season was, indeed, college football's team of the year. And, should the program continue to progress under Saban's direction, this is the team that will be hailed as the one that began Alabama's return to glory.

TOMMY DEAS
Executive Sports Editor
The Tuscaloosa News